SCHOLASTIC GUIDES

# HOW TO WRITE
# POETRY

# SCHOLASTIC GUIDES
# HOW TO WRITE
# POETRY

## PAUL B. JANECZKO

SCHOLASTIC INC.
New York  Toronto  London  Auckland  Sydney
Mexico City  New Delhi  Hong Kong

Sincere thanks to Sarah Sabasteanski,
my "research assistant" and e-mail buddy,
for answering all my questions.

*Library of Congress Cataloging-in-Publication Data*
Janeczko, Paul B. • How to write poetry / Paul B. Janeczko • p. cm.
— (Scholastic guides) • Includes bibliographical references and index.
Summary: Provides practical advice with checklists on the art of writing poetry.
ISBN 0-590-10078-5 (paperback)
1. Poetry—Authorship—Juvenile literature. [1. Poetry—Authorship.] I. Title.
II. Series. PN1059.A9J36 1999 808.1—dc21 98-26866 CIP AC
10 9 8 7 6      02 03 04 05

Printed in the U.S.A. 23
First trade paperback printing, April 2001

*Book design by Nancy Sabato*
*Composition by Brad Walrod*

*With affection and admiration,*
*this book is for*
*Susan Bean, Connie Burns, and Karen Guter,*
*who love kids and love words.*

P.B.J.

# CONTENTS

# INTRODUCTION

ONE OF THE QUESTIONS THAT COMES UP ALL THE TIME when I talk to young writers is, "Why did you start writing poetry?" It's a good question and one that I've thought about quite a bit. I started writing poetry when I realized that some of the things I wanted to say could best be said in poetry. Poetry is special. Like a lot of writing I do, writing poetry is fun. Don't get me wrong. Writing anything well takes hard work, but there is still the element of enjoyment running through it like silver through the side of a mountain. But the kick I get from writing a good poem is different.

The first poems I recall writing were haiku that I wrote in college. In graduate school I wrote more poems in different forms. I fell in love and wrote about how *wonderful* the girl was and how *wonderful* I felt when I was with her. I fell out of love and wrote poems about how unfair life was, how miserable I felt. Now, when I look back at those poems, I can see ways that I could make some of them better. (Most are beyond help!) Even though the poems may not have been very good, they gave me the chance to explore my feelings in concrete and vivid language. That is part of the power of poetry. Writing poetry gives you the chance to fall in love with language again and again.

# CHAPTER ONE
## GETTING READY

"WHERE DO YOU GET YOUR IDEAS?" I'VE HEARD THAT question from students and adults more times than I can count. I'm afraid that many people feel that writers have some special access to ideas that other people don't have. Like some 800-number that supplies ideas if you have your credit card handy! But that's simply not true.

### FINDING IDEAS AND SAVING THEM

Most writers will tell you the same thing about ideas: They are all around you. However, if you want to write, you need to look and listen carefully. You also need to save your ideas. If you don't, there is a good chance that they will slip away from you like quarters at an arcade. Good ideas do not, of course, guarantee good writing. That takes hard work, imagination, and a willingness to take chances.

There are lots of ways to save your ideas. An obvious place is in a pocket notebook. (Don't leave home without it!) It should be small enough to fit into your pocket or backpack but thick enough to give you plenty of wide-open spaces to write down your observations and thoughts. When I drive in my car, even on short trips around town, I always carry a microcassette tape recorder with me. It didn't take me long to realize that to drive and write notes at the same time is dumb. So, if I get an idea while I'm in my car, I can easily push the record button and save my ideas on a tape and play it back whenever I have time.

I am guilty of saving ideas in odd places—old napkins, backs of envelopes, on the palm of my hand—but, like most writers, I've come to realize that it is best to keep my ideas in a book. That's why my journal is invaluable. I recommend that if you are serious about writing, you give some thought to keeping a journal or a writer's notebook. Although a journal is a great place to jot down brilliant ideas, it can be much more than that.

WRITING TIP FROM A POET

My journal is the heart of my writing. There I record dreams, memories, funny happenings and wild ideas. Free to play, I write in different directions and colors; I draw; I tape in leaves, notes from kids, boarding passes. From such compost, poems, stories and even novels grow.

George Ella Lyon

What *is* a journal? Good question. Some people think it's a book in which you write things that happened to you each day. But if that's a journal, what's a diary? Another good question. So maybe before you can decide if you want to keep a journal, you need to know the difference between a diary and a journal.

For starters, both are, of course, books that you write in. But since a diary usually has a space for each day of the year, it comes with the expectation that you will write something each day and that your writing will be limited to the space provided for that day.

A journal is different. With a journal there are no expectations to write something every day. Nor is there any space limitation. You can write as often as you like in a journal. You can write a few sentences or many pages. And a journal can hold more than just writing. You might think of it as a gigantic shoe box that can hold all sorts of treasures and memories. It can be a best friend. It can be a mirror to help you see yourself. It can be a mailbox where you store letters. It can be a sketchbook and a photo album. A journal can be a combination of all these things.

Remember that your journal is *your* book, so it should reflect you and your personality. It is a place to express yourself. If you like to paint, you might think of it as a blank canvas. If you like to write, you might think of it as . . . well, as a lot of blank pages. A journal can be different things for you.

- It can be a place for you to experiment with words, lines, colors, and shapes.
- It can be a place where you write things that you can't (or don't want to) write for a class assignment.
- It can record the story of your life or the history of your family and friends.
- It can be a place to collect quotations that are funny or inspirational; quotations from novels, poems, comedians,

and friends that show the power of our magnificent language.

- It can be a place where you save your deepest confessions. Likewise, it can be a place for you to figure out a problem.
- It can be a place to write letters to mail as well as letters that will remain in your journal. Letters to yourself, to people you will never see again, to people you love, to people with whom you are in heated disagreement.
- It can be an album of photos of family, friends, places you've enjoyed, people you admire, and people you'd like to meet.
- It can be a sketchbook for your drawings, paintings, and doodles.

But no matter what you put in your journal, it should be a place where you can freely explore your creativity. A place where you can comfortably take a close look at your personality, hopes, and fears. A place where you can be *you*.

WRITING TIP FROM A POET

I often get my ideas from juxtapositions of unusual things—something clicks inside my head, and I take note. It's like the exercise where you're supposed to pick out the one thing in a list that doesn't belong—I pick it out, then write about how it got there.

Jim Daniels

## A Word About Privacy

Although you can let anyone look at your journal, most people want to keep their journals private. But there are few things more tempting than a journal left unattended. The best way to keep your journal private is to be sure it's not a temptation for someone else. In other words, hide it. That doesn't mean you have to pry up a floorboard and stash it underfoot. But it might mean keeping it out of sight in a closet, in your backpack, or at the bottom of one of your drawers. Some people write a brief message at the beginning of the journal to those who might find the book, accidentally or not. Something like: *You have picked up my personal journal. Please respect my privacy and return the journal to me without reading it. Thank you.* While this sort of message will work with honorable people, others may simply ignore it. So, the best advice is to keep your journal out of sight of anyone who might be tempted to read it.

## The Right Tools

Any good craftsperson will tell you that to do a job right you need the right tools. The same is true for your journal. Since you are hoping that your journal will be your longtime companion, you want to make sure that you get the tools with which you will feel comfortable.

✦ **A Book**  You have many different possibilities when you are looking for the book to use as a journal. Walk into any good stationery store or discount store and you will find many books to choose from. Which is the right one? That's easy: the one that feels most comfortable for you. Some people like a large sketchbook with big, snow-white pages. Other journal writers (like me) have got to have lines on their pages. You might prefer a basic spiral notebook. Some writers I know use a three-ring binder because they feel it gives them greater flexibility to move the pages around. And you can take a stack of composition paper with you and leave the binder at home. You might like a stenography pad. I like to use those composition books with the black-and-white marbleized covers. The point is simple: Choose a book that *feels* right for you.

✦ PENS AND MARKERS    I am a pen freak. I love the feel of a good pen, usually a fountain pen. I love the way the ink flows so smoothly from a quality fountain pen. Many of my friends think I am crazy to care so much about a pen. They are happy to settle for a simple ballpoint pen with a gnawed end. I say they don't know what they're missing. As with the notebook, you must pick a pen that feels good to you. It might be a fountain pen or a felt-tip marker that writes blue or a ballpoint pen that writes green or even a pencil. It's strictly your choice.

In addition to a pen, you might want some colored pencils and markers to jazz up your writing. Maybe some highlighters to emphasize some words, phrases, or ideas in your writing. You might also use highlighters to draw a connection between ideas. For example, when you reread your journal, you might notice that your boyfriend or parents are mentioned a lot. One way to keep track of such a subject is to highlight it with a yellow marker. Or, you might highlight in pink every time you have an idea or see an image that might be the start of a poem.

## The Right Time and Place

One of the wonderful things about a journal is you can write in it whenever you like. And wherever you like. Having said that, however, it is a good idea to think about setting aside a special time and place to write in your journal. Again, what works for you is best. Because I usually wake up before my wife and daughter, I sometimes take advantage of that quiet morning time to write in my journal. On other days, I write in my journal when I am finished working for the day. What's a good time for you to write in your journal? At the end of school? Before dinner? Before you turn off the light at night?

As far as a place is concerned, I prefer to write at a desk or at a table. Other people feel just as comfortable writing propped up in bed or sprawled on the sofa. Do you have "your place" where you feel most comfortable? It might be a place where you go when you want to shut out the world. Your room? The tree house you used to play in? A quiet corner of the library? You can write in your journal anyplace, but finding "your place" helps make the whole process special.

## A Checklist of Pitfalls

To help you get the most out of your journal and maintain a sense of enjoyment when you write, let me offer some suggestions. It will be helpful if you remind yourself of these things from time to time, particularly when you find yourself dreading your journal as if it were some big, hairy dog with bad breath coming to slobber in your face.

✓ *It's okay if you don't write in your journal every day.* Or, even every other day, for that matter. The journal is there to serve you, not to be your master. When you feel guilty because you haven't written in your journal for a few days, it is time to repeat this suggestion to yourself over and over until you believe it. Write in your journal when you have something to say or something to add to the book.

✓ *Never criticize what you write.* One of the biggest obstacles for writers who want to experiment with their language is that nasty voice most of us have that tells us that what we are doing is stupid, not very good, or a flat-out waste of time. You know the voice. Yours might whisper to you. Mine is shrill, like a rusty nail being yanked out of a plank. Don't listen to that voice. Your journal is yours. What you write or draw won't be perfect. But it doesn't have to be. It just has to be honest.

✓ *Neatness doesn't count.* It's okay if you make mistakes in your journal. When you do, don't be afraid to cross them out. Draw arrows if you find a section that belongs somewhere else. If you drop a blob of catsup on a page, wipe it up and write around the pink stain. If you are too worried about keeping a "perfect" journal, you may be too afraid to take a chance. And it's only when you take a chance with your writing that you will learn what you can do.

✓ *Spelling doesn't count.* If your journal becomes the kind of book it can be, there will be times when you will be writing so fast that you won't want to stop to consider spelling rules. Fine. If spelling mistakes in your journal bother you that much, go back and correct them later. But don't dampen a burst of enthusiasm to grab a dictionary.

✓ *Don't throw out anything.* Keep everything that you write in your journal. You never know what will come of it. I can't tell you how many times early in my career I nearly tossed out a pile of notes because I thought they were worthless, only to later realize that in all that junk there were a couple of ideas worth hanging on to.

✓ *Date every entry.* Since one of the reasons to keep a journal is to record your life, it's helpful to know, for example, when you thought about the value of friendship or when you were feeling elated or left out. If you look back over your journal, dated entries may help you see a pattern or notice recurring themes in your life.

✓ *Your journal is for you.* You are certainly free to share your journal entries with whomever you choose. Your girlfriend, for example. However, be careful that you do not wind up writing things for someone else. When you know that someone else is going to read your journal, you may not be as honest as you would be if the book was for your eyes only. Always remember that your journal is just that: *your* journal.

Nothing takes the place of keeping a journal, in which to record observations and thoughts, a phrase, a word, an idea that can be used when there is leisure to write; nor is there any substitute for observation: the time taken to carefully examine and respond to the world around us.

Myra Cohn Livingston

## READING

While you are capturing your thoughts and experiences in your journal, don't forget that you cannot be a good writer—poet or prose writer—if you are not a reader. So, make that one of the things you do whenever you have a few spare minutes: Read some poems. All kinds of poems. Rhyming and non-rhyming poems. Short poems. Long poems. Only by reading what other poets have written will you be able to get some sense of what your poems can be like. At first, you will copy the poets you admire. That's fine. Everybody does it when they're beginning. But as you write more poems, you will gain more confidence in your own talent and ability, and you will rely less on imitating the work of other poets. Even when you are on your own as a poet, it will be important for you to keep reading poetry.

If you're not sure where to find books of good poems, you're in luck. Throughout this guide I've scattered the titles of some poetry books that I think you will enjoy. Beyond that, I've included a longer list of poetry books at the end of the guide.

Don't limit yourself to the books on that list. Go to the library and cruise the poetry section. You may be surprised by what you discover. I can't count the times I've browsed the stacks and discovered some wonderful poets, who were, at the time, unknown to me.

When you take a book of poems and start reading, don't feel that you have to like or understand every poem you read. That's not going to happen. And it's okay if you don't like a lot of what you read. Just ask yourself why you don't like a poem. What did the poet do or not do that put you off? Was it the subject? Was it the language? Didn't you like the fact that the poem rhymed? Or didn't rhyme? By answering these kinds of questions, you will begin to develop your own sense of what makes a good poem. And, as you write, you will try to make sure that your poem reflects what you have learned from other poets.

This book will not, of course, teach you everything you need to know about writing poetry. That's not its purpose. Rather, as the title suggests, these pages will serve as a guide for you, i.e., something that points you in the right direction and helps you avoid some of the pitfalls of writing. Like any other art, poetry writing takes practice. The more you practice and think about what you are writing, the more you read poems and books about writing poetry, the better your poems will become.

Notice that I said this book is meant to be a guide for writing poems, not a blueprint. There are no rigid blueprints for writing good poems. No follow-these-steps-and-you-get-a-good-poem, although some rhyming poems follow a specific form. Good writing of any kind takes trial and error. In some ways it's like taking a trip. You know where you want to go, and you think you know the route you will take. But once you get on the road, you may run into detours, dead ends, side trips, and pit stops for rest. Eventually, you will arrive at your destination, but you will have had a more adventurous time of it.

Sometimes when you write a poem, you may think you know what the poem is going to be. But as you write and tinker your way through several drafts, you find that the poem wants to be something else. Maybe you thought you wanted to write a poem about a party, but the poem wound up being about friendship. As a writer, you must learn to trust your intuition. When a poem wants to go its own way, let it. See where it takes you. You may be pleasantly surprised.

So, if you're ready to write some poems, sharpen your pencil, grab your journal, and let your imagination loose!

---

### WRITING TIP FROM A POET

Poetry is a secret kingdom. If you engage all your senses—seeing, touching, listening, smelling, and tasting—the gates open. Seemingly unimportant things begin to speak: salmon-colored geraniums, a smooth beach stone, your mother's voice when she calls your name, the diesel smell of the school bus, and that first bite of a Snickers bar. Details are the beginnings of poetry and the doors to your kingdom.

Christine Hemp

## SOMETHING TO READ

If you want more sound advice about writing poetry, check out these books:

- *Gonna Bake Me a Rainbow Poem*, Peter Sears, Scholastic, 1990.
- *Knock at a Star: a Child's Introduction to Poetry*, X.J. Kennedy and Dorothy M. Kennedy, Little, Brown, 1985.
- *The Place My Words Are Looking For*, edited by Paul B. Janeczko, Bradbury Press, 1990.
- *Poem-Making: Ways to Begin Writing Poetry*, Myra C. Livingston, HarperCollins, 1991.

# CHAPTER TWO
## STARTING TO WRITE

As you fill your journal with lots of good stuff—things that are important or fascinating to you—you're that much closer to writing some poems. The things and feelings you can write poems about are all around you and inside you. A poet is, in some ways, like a scientist. They both observe and report. True, the form of their reports will be different—a poet writes a poem and a scientist writes a prose report—but the process they go through is frequently the same.

## THE WRITING PROCESS

Although it varies from writer to writer and even from one piece of writing to the next, the writing process usually involves the same steps:

- Brainstorming, when you doodle and jot down ideas, thoughts, feelings, and images;
- Drafting, when you take your first crack at the poem;
- Editing, when you go over your poem and look and listen for ways to make it better;
- Revising, when you make improvements in your poem;

⚒ Publishing, when your poem is complete and you decide it's time to share it with someone.

The process is never exactly the same. And there is no set time for the process to play itself out. On occasion, you have probably written a poem in a short time, with only a little editing and revising. Other poems may have taken you much longer to write. If you're lucky, you have a trusted reader who can help the process by listening to a new poem and offering some comments and suggestions.

Let me share one example of how the writing process worked for me. I wasn't thinking about writing a poem. I was simply driving on a country road past a farmhouse and saw a man and a dog walking across a pasture. I thought I spotted some sort of flower on the front porch. The skies had darkened and I could almost feel the approaching storm. I was struck enough by the scene that I pulled onto the shoulder of the road and whipped out my pen and small notebook. I quickly jotted down some notes, enough to save the scene.

When I got home, I took my jottings and used them to recreate the scene in my mind. Then I brainstormed a list of details:

- man and dog walking through pasture
- white farmhouse in distance
- black or brown dog barking
- dark thunderclouds
- lightning flashing
- rain pouring down

- wash on the line, flapping
- grayish sky
- like the ocean
- bright flower in window (like a lighthouse?)

As I looked over the list, I tried again to visualize the scene. Then I grabbed a pen and a pad of paper and began doing what poets do all the time: looking for the best way to create a vivid image that would bring the scene to life for a reader. Over time I created what I considered to be a good poem. At that point I put the poem away in a folder, where it rested out of sight for a few weeks. When I looked at the poem again, I saw problems that I had not seen in the rush of enthusiasm that often goes with a first draft. So, I took some more time to edit, revise, and tinker with my poem before I wound up with a version that satisfied me:

### LIGHTNING RIDES

Lightning rides
the sea slate sky,
dog follows master
over crests of pasture.
In a window
of the white farmhouse,
a beacon:
a single geranium.

What I wanted to do in the poem was create an image of the scene I had seen that afternoon. To make sure the image was clear, I had to make sure I used vivid words. So, for instance, I wrote *sea slate sky* instead of settling for simply comparing the color to the ocean. Quite by accident, I saw that I could use terms usually associated with the ocean to stitch the poem together: *sea slate sky, over crests of pasture, a beacon.*

It's important to remind you that I did not set out to write a poem that would describe a farmhouse setting in terms of the ocean. I merely wanted to vividly describe the scene I had seen. It was through the process of writing that I discovered the magic of this poem.

## ACROSTIC POEMS

For your first poem, try writing an acrostic about a subject that you know very well: yourself. If you've done a lot of writing in your journal, you probably have learned quite a bit about yourself. This poem will give you a chance to use some of that information. Here are some acrostic poems that students of mine wrote to introduce themselves to me:

JOSH
Jokes
Oranges
Spaghetti
Holy cow!

## LAUREN

**L**oves her mom
**A**lso likes to cook
**U**nlikes to clean her room
**R**uins some things
**E**ats a lot
**N**onlikes spaghetti

## KURT

**K**ind most of the time.
**U**sually
**R**ely on my shooting video games
**T**o take out my anger

You noticed that the subject of each poem is a person, the poet. That subject is the title of each poem. But also note how each letter of the title is the first letter of each line of the poem. You can write an acrostic poem with a single word in each line, or you can have longer lines. It all depends on what you have to say.

Begin your draft by writing your name at the top of a page in your journal. Make a list of some important things about yourself. Think of some of the things you would tell someone who was interested in getting to know you better. You might want to include your likes and dislikes. Some of your personality traits. Interesting comments about yourself. Be honest. Remember that you don't need to show this poem to anyone.

A pitfall to avoid is staring at the letters of your name and wondering what in the world you can possibly say about yourself that would begin with that letter. If you try to write your poem that way, you will, most likely, wind up doing more sitting and staring than writing. Rather, think of what you want to say about yourself. Look at the list of things about yourself that you brainstormed. Look for ways you can work those ideas into the letters of your name.

As you work on your acrostic poem, you might want to keep this checklist in mind:

✓ You can write your acrostic poem as a list, with a different item on each line.

✓ Or, you can write your poem as a sentence or two that continue through the poem, like "Kurt."

✓ Your poem can also be a combination of these two possibilities.

✓ Make sure you have selected items that capture the essence of your subject.

✓ The first letter of each line must come from the title or subject of your poem.

Remember that you can, of course, write an acrostic poem about any subject. All you need to do is substitute the subject for your name and write the poem as you did the one about yourself. It can be about someone or something concrete and real—friend, father, soccer, Mozart—or it can be about something abstract, like love, loneliness, or friendship. If you write about something abstract like love, make sure your poem *shows* love with specific examples.

**Try This** . . . When you have had time to tinker with your draft and think you have a good poem, try writing another, perhaps with a different slant or emphasis. Your first acrostic poem might be about your total personality. Try writing one that emphasizes your likes. Perhaps, for example, you might write one that reflects your love of sports or reading. You might write an acrostic poem about your role in the family. If you are an only child or the oldest child, how can you write a poem about that role? Or, think about how you would change your name if you could, then write an acrostic about that name.

◆　◆　◆

SOMETHING TO READ

✦ *Autumn: An Alphabet Acrostic* (Clarion Books, 1997) by Steven Schnur is a collection of well-crafted acrostic poems that captures the sights and sounds of the season.

Poetry is sound. It's a lot of other things, too, of course, like structure and meaning and rhythm, but sound cannot be ignored when you are writing a poem. Not only the sound of individual words, but the sounds the words make when they are together on the page. You are trying to create a music with the words in your poem. It might be sweet music or it might be harsh music, but you must have your ears open when you write (and read) poetry.

If you've never really given much thought to the sound of words, I suggest you start collecting words. Save a few pages of your journal for your word collection. You'll be making what I call a Poet's Wordbank. What words should you collect? That's up to you, but I suggest you start with your favorite words. My list of favorite words is long, but here are a few at the top of that list: *ointment, hawkweed, contraption, billow,* and *siesta*. What are your favorite words? Words you like the sound of. Words that give you an image. Write your list in your journal.

You can makes columns of words in your journal. You can find interesting words in newspapers and magazines and paste them in your journal. Look in atlases, nature books, computer books, seed catalogs, prayer books, and art books. Make all sorts of wild combinations: *Picasso's hard drive, pink river, yawning mushrooms*. Read the words aloud. Listen to the sounds. You can make a collage or a mobile with the cut-out words. Or, write them on file cards, which will allow you to share and swap them with friends. Listen to the sounds. You can use some of the words in your Poet's Wordbank.

Will collecting words make you a better poet? Not necessarily. But it could very well make you more attentive to the sounds of words, and you cannot be a good poet without that. So, start collecting. There's no rush or deadline. Just keep your eyes and ears open and keep some space free in your journal for the words you collect.

📖 *Try This* . . . Before you read another word, open your journal to a fresh page and write down some of your favorite words. Don't stop to think or analyze your choices. Just write.

◆   ◆   ◆

## SOUND EFFECTS

As you listen closely to words—those you say and those you write—you'll hear how words sometimes follow patterns to create sounds. Although there is a long list of terms related to sound in poetry, you should be aware of three basic terms:

▓ Alliteration is the repetition of the initial consonants of words. If you have ever tried to get through a tongue twister, you've used alliteration. For example, *Peter Piper picked a peck of pickled peppers* is an example of alliteration.

Other examples are such phrases as *setting sun, totally terrible territory, nasty nonsense*, and *far-flung favorite*. Examples of alliteration abound in poetry. See how Samuel Taylor Coleridge used alliteration when he wrote, "So fierce a foe to frenzy." One of my favorite couplets, written by British poet Alexander Pope, happens to be full of alliteration:

> The bookful blockhead, ignorantly read,
> With loads of learned lumber in his head.

- Assonance is the repetition of the vowel sounds in words. For example, note the *oo* sound in *zoom, loon*, and *ruin* or the *ee* sound in *heat, three*, and *meet*. Notice how John Masefield used assonance in this line: "Slow the low gradual moan came in the snowing." Can you hear the *o* sound in four words? Assonance occurs frequently in the work of a master poet such as William Shakespeare, so it is easy to find many examples. Here's one: "Shall ever medicine thee to that sweet sleep."

- Onomatopoeia is a word that makes the sound of the action it describes. For example, *thump, bang, honk, moo, ring*, and *hiss*. In a sense, these words make their own sound effects. Robert Burns wrote how "The birds sit chittering in the thorn." Describing branches covered with ice, Robert Frost wrote that "they click upon themselves."

◆ ◆ ◆

## REPETITION

The sound devices described above can help hold a poem together and create music. Repetition can serve the same purpose. You have noticed how this is particularly true of many of the songs you hear on the radio, many of which have words and lines repeated. This is nothing new. Early ballads used repetition effectively, especially refrain, the exact repetition of words or phrases. Edgar Allan Poe's famous poem about the death of his young wife begins with this stanza, or group of lines:

It was many and many a year ago,
    In a kingdom by the sea,
That a maiden there lived whom you may know
    By the name of ANNABEL LEE;
And this maiden she lived with no other thought
    Than to love and be loved by me.

In each of the six stanzas of the poem, Poe repeats his dead wife's name at least once (in capital letters, no less) to emphasize how deep his love was and how great his loss. Notice how the repetition at the end of the fifth and into the final stanza adds to the power of the poem:

And neither the angels in heaven above,
    Nor the demons down under the sea,
Can ever dissever my soul from the soul
    Of the beautiful ANNABEL LEE:


For the moon never beams, without bringing me dreams
    Of the beautiful ANNABEL LEE:
And the stars never rise, but I feel the bright eyes
    Of the beautiful ANNABEL LEE:
And so, all the night-tide, I lie down by the side
Of my darling—my darling—my life and my bride,
    In the sepulchre there by the sea—
    In her tomb by the sounding sea.

EDGAR ALLAN POE


Warning: There is a danger in overusing any of the sound techniques, of using them simply to show off. So, when you use alliteration, for example, make sure that you have a good reason for doing so. And if you use a refrain, make sure you are repeating something that is important to your poem. Otherwise, you run the risk of boring your reader to the point where she will not finish reading your poem.

## Something to Listen To

Your school or public library may have recordings of poets reading their work. Check some out and give a listen to the magic of the words. Here are a few suggestions to get you started:

- *How to Eat a Poem*, Eve Merriam, Harper Audio, 1990.
- *The Butterfly Jar*, Jeff Moss, Bantam Audio, 1992.
- *The Dragons Are Singing Tonight*, Jack Prelutsky, who even sings his poems, Listening Library, 1994.
- *The Best of Michael Rosen*, by the hilarious British poet, Wetlands Press, 1995.

# CHAPTER THREE
# WRITING POEMS THAT RHYME

NOW THAT YOU'VE HAD A CHANCE TO WARM UP A BIT BY writing some acrostic poems, you might want to try writing some poems that rhyme. The three short poems that follow—synonym poem, opposite, and clerihew—will let you work with rhythm and rhyme as you compose some humorous short poems.

## SYNONYM POEMS

A synonym poem is as short as a rhyming poem can be: two lines. (You do know what a synonym is, right? Just in case you don't know, a synonym is a word that means the same thing or almost the same thing as another word.) When you have two lines of poetry that rhyme, it's called a couplet, so each synonym poem is made up of one couplet. Read these synonym poems and see if you can tell how these poems are written:

> SCHOOL LUNCH
> Burgers, prunes, and warm spaghetti
> To eat this stuff I'm not ready

### THIN
Scrawny, slender, skinny, slight
Your plump friends tell you you're too light

### WEIRD
Bizarre, strange, and spooky things
Books and stories by Stephen King

### OUTLAW
Pirate, bandit, thief, or crook
At them the judge should throw the book

Look over this checklist of things to keep in mind when you write your synonym poem:

✓ Each poem is made up of two lines of poetry that rhyme.

✓ The title is the subject of the poem.

✓ The first line contains three or four synonyms for the subject.

✓ The second line of each poem can do one of two things: it can describe the subject a little more, as in "Weird," or it can tell how the poet feels about the subject, as in "School Lunch."

✓ Each line generally has seven or eight syllables arranged in a way that gives the poem its rhythm. If you're not sure what the rhythm of these poems is, read the examples out loud without the titles. You will hear the rhythm.

✓ A synonym poem can be funny.

Before you start drafting your synonym poem, do some brainstorming on paper. When you know what you want to write about, put that word at the top of a journal page. Since a synonym poem is essentially a descriptive poem, a good subject will be something that you can describe. Maybe a person, place, or thing. But it could also be an emotion—anger, joy, or sadness, for example—or an adjective—such as tall, heavy, or round.

Once you have a good subject, make a list of words that are synonyms for that word. Feel free to use a thesaurus from the library or one that is part of a word processing program for your computer. A thesaurus, a book that lists and may define synonyms and antonyms for other words, is a wonderful storehouse of great words that we often know but might not be able to think of when we need them. (And isn't "thesaurus" an interesting word? I picture some sort of vegetarian dinosaur.)

When your list has a dozen or so words, look for the ones that will make up your first line of poetry. Write them out. How do they sound together? Do they work with each other to make a suitable rhythm? Or, do they quarrel with one another and sound as if they don't quite belong in the same line? If that's the case, you might simply need to move a couple of words around within the line. Sometimes that helps the rhythm. If moving some words doesn't help, go back to your list to find substitutes.

When you have a first line that sings a slick song for you, look for a good second line that will complete your poem. Remember that your second line will describe the subject a little more or tell how you feel about it. And, don't forget the rhythm of the poem. If you're not sure how your poem sounds, read it out loud. You will hear things when you read something aloud that you may very well miss when you read it silently. Even if you know your poem sounds good, read it out loud for the sheer joy of hearing the words work together so smoothly.

Try This . . . Once you've written a couple of good synonym poems, you might want to write a cycle of poems, three or four poems that are somehow related. For example, you could write a cycle of synonym poems about sports, the seasons, members of your family, or your friends. Because these poems are so short, they are perfect to put on a card, maybe with a drawing, and send to someone. You could send your best friend a synonym poem for her birthday. Or, wouldn't your parents be surprised if you wrote a poem about them and gave it to them on their anniversary!

◆　◆　◆

WRITING TIP FROM A POET

Some teachers think kids never should rhyme, because rhymes can sound too forced: "My reindeer/drinks brain beer," or something. Yet, I've seen kids' poems containing wonderful rhymes: wish/squish, pewter/computer. Like learning to play the piano, rhyming takes practice. But if you want to, why shouldn't you start?

X.J. Kennedy

## OPPOSITES

An opposite is another descriptive poem that is, well, the opposite of a synonym poem. You might even call it an antonym poem. (An antonym is a word that means the opposite of another word. Some obvious antonyms are *good/evil* and *high/low*.) One difference between a synonym poem and an opposite is that in an opposite you describe something by what it's not. Confused? Maybe some examples will help you. As you read these poems, see if you can tell what makes a good opposite:

What is the opposite of kind?
A goat that butts you from behind.

The opposite of chair
Is sitting down with nothing there.

What is the opposite of new?
It might be stale gum that's hard to chew,
A hotdog roll as hard as a rock,
Or a soiled and smelly forgotten sock.

You can probably see right away that opposites are more challenging than synonym poems. But, as the challenge increases, so does the potential for more enjoyment when you write a good poem. Here is a checklist of the ingredients of a good opposite:

✓ It is, obviously, about opposites.

✓ It is written in couplets. But, where the synonym poem can only be one couplet—two rhymed lines—the opposite can be two, four, six, eight, ten lines, or more, as long as you write it in couplets.

✓ An opposite will frequently, though not always, begin with the question: *What is the opposite of* _____? If you decide to start your poem with a question, the rest of the poem will answer that question. However, as the examples show, you could also begin your poem with something like: *The opposite of* _____ *is* _____.

✓ Like any well-crafted piece of writing, a good opposite will contain specific details, not simply generalities.

✓ Although the rhythm of an opposite is not as predictable as the rhythm of a synonym poem, you must make sure that your poem does have its own music.

You can begin an opposite the same way you started to write your synonym poem, although you may find that you spend more time trying to find a good subject because not everything has an opposite. For example, encyclopedia. In addition to being a tough word to rhyme with, finding its opposite will be tough. So, take some time to brainstorm some things, persons, and feelings that truly do have opposites. For example, school, your sister, or anger might be a good subject for you. Sometimes it helps to use an adjective as a subject. Words such as *happy, dreary, short,* and *cozy* are begging to be used in an opposite. Write good subjects for opposites in your journal. A good idea is like a good friend. You never can have enough.

When you find a good subject for an opposite, write it at the top of a fresh page of your journal. Then start writing down ideas that are the opposite of your subject. *Do not* (I repeat: *do not*) look for words that will rhyme with your subject. If you do, you will worry too much about rhyme instead of about what your poem says. Trust me: Once you have a list of good opposite words, you'll find the rhyme you need.

When you start the draft of your first opposite, I suggest that you make it easy on yourself and begin with the question, *What is the opposite of _____?* After all, that could be half of your poem! However, after you have written a rhyming second line, you need to ask yourself if the poem is complete. Some two-line opposites are simply not finished. For example:

What is the opposite of school?
It would be something very cool.

What is the opposite of tall?
I'd say it's something small.

Can you hear how these poems need another couple of lines to finish the job? They are good starts, but they are lacking the specific details that a good poem will always have. (In your journal, you might want to write additional couplets that would complete these too-short opposites.)

Try This . . . Don't be satisfied writing all two-line opposites. While they certainly are fun to write, push yourself to look for more specifics that are the opposite of your subject. Challenge yourself to write a four-line opposite and even a six- or eight-line opposite. It'll take patience and work, but you will have every reason to be proud of yourself when you write a clever opposite of six or eight lines.

◆　◆　◆

SOMETHING TO READ

If you want to read some wonderful opposites, go to your library and look for:

⚜ *Opposites* and *More Opposites* by Richard Wilbur, Harcourt Brace, 1973 and 1991.

# POETCRAFT: CREATING IMAGES

When you write a poem you are trying to create an image (or a series of images) that will help the reader to experience what you experienced. You may want to put the reader in a scene, real or imaginary. You might want the person to feel an emotion the way you felt it. You are going for the total effect of your words.

One way to help the reader connect with your poem is to include details that appeal to the senses: sight, sound, smell, taste, and touch. That's not to say that you are going to include all the senses in every poem you write. But it does mean that you need to be aware of which senses you need to explore to make your poem a vivid reading experience. Since we live in a visual culture—we watch TV and movies, read books and magazines—we tend to think of an image as visual, while ignoring the other senses. There are a number of ways to create strong images, but they all ask that you use vivid, specific language.

You can create clear images by using strong verbs. If I said to you, "My friend went down the street," I would be guilty of using a weak verb: *went*. Can you think of other verbs that more accurately show how my friend "went" down the street? How about these possibilities:

My friend *ran* down the street.

My friend *wobbled* down the street.

My friend *hopped* down the street.

My friend *danced* down the street.

My friend *sprinted* down the street.

Each of these verbs gives a different picture of how my friend "went" down the street, doesn't it? Can you think of other strong verbs you can use instead of "went"?

**Try This . . .** On a page of your journal, write down some vivid verbs that you could use in place of the weak verbs listed below. Pick verbs that create an image.

said

looked

moved

gave

hit

When you have given your list some thought, look up these verbs in the thesaurus and see what other strong verbs you can find. Add them all to your Poet's Wordbank.

❖    ❖    ❖

What about your adjectives? Can you find a more precise way to say, "The car was *blue*"? You could make a comparison and say, "The car was *as blue as a robin's egg*." Or, you could check a thesaurus to find that some other words for blue are: *azure, sapphire, aquamarine, turquoise, navy, lapis lazuli,* and *indigo*. These words are not interchangeable, of course, but that is the point. Each of them describes a more specific variation of blue.

**Try This . . .** Check a thesaurus and find synonyms for these words:

    mad
    silly
    glowing
    rapid
    pleasant

If you're not sure of the exact meaning of some of the synonyms, look them up in a good dictionary. Add the best words to your Poet's Wordbank.

◆ ◆ ◆

WRITING TIP FROM A POET

When you write a poem, you are like a magician conjuring up mental pictures in the mind of your reader. So choose your words carefully. The word daisy will evoke a sharper image than the word flower. The word birch will bring to mind a different picture than the word tree. Seagull or eagle will conjure up mental scenes that are totally different from those brought on by the word bird. When I hear the word cardinal I think of the bright red ones that come to my feeder in the winter.

WHAT'S IN A WORD?
Say "bird,"
and a sparrow appears

inside you and ruffles
its feathers.

Say "cardinal,"
and the bird turns red.
Suddenly it is winter.
With a lot of snow. And look!
There are sunflower seeds
in the feeder.

Siv Cedering

## CLERIHEWS

During World War II, a man by the name of E. C. Bentley wrote a regular column for a London newspaper. In that column he included short rhyming poems about historical and literary figures, written in a form that he had invented when he was a student. And, since his middle name was Clerihew, that's what he called this new type of poem. Here's one that he wrote:

Edgar Allan Poe
Was passionately fond of roe.     [fish eggs]
He always liked to chew some
When writing anything gruesome.

E. C. BENTLEY

And here are a couple that were written by student writers:

That famous lady, Mona Lisa
Whose smile has been a real teasa
Will never tell this world we're in
What's behind her fabled grin.

Basketball ace, Dr. J
Is seven feet tall so they say.
His only hang up is buying shoes.
But that's why they invented canoes.

When you begin to draft your first clerihew, keep the items on this checklist in mind:

✓ A clerihew is about a celebrity.

✓ It pokes gentle fun at that person, so it tends to be humorous. (Please do not write mean-spirited clerihew. That's not what these poems are about.)

✓ It is always made up of two couplets.

✓ The first line ends with a person's name, so you must rhyme with that name. (The first line of Bentley's clerihew contains only the name of the subject. But, if you'd like, you can begin your first line with a couple of words that identify the subject. In other words, your first line should not be something like, *There once was the Mona Lisa*.)

As usual, before you start writing, brainstorm some good subjects for your poems. You can start by listing some categories of celebrities. For example, movie stars, athletes, characters in books, and rock musicians. Next, write down the names of specific people in those categories, trying to include people who have some quality or characteristic you can poke fun at. It might be a basketball player's shaved head or a movie starlet's behavior in public. Jot down some things you think you'd like to say about your subject.

Once you have zeroed in on a good subject, start drafting your poem. The first line is the easy one because you know it must end with the celebrity's name. The other lines will be more challenging, but also more fun to write. Remember to have fun with your clerihew. Because you must rhyme with a person's name, this is a good time to try out some outrageous rhymes.

When you've completed your draft, read your clerihew out loud. How does it sound? Is it smooth and graceful? If it's not, take a careful look at the poem and see what you can do to improve the rhythm. Can you make it smoother by changing a word or two? (Check your thesaurus.) Or, perhaps major surgery is needed. Don't worry about it. That's what rewriting is all about: finding a way to make your writing better.

Try This . . . If you've written about a contemporary person, why not put your poem on a poster with a magazine picture of your subject? Or, you can draw a caricature of the celebrity. You could even do a series of poem posters about people in the same field, say, NBA superstars or rap singers.

◆　◆　◆

## SOMETHING TO READ

Although many of Bentley's clerihews are dated and very British, you can find all of them in *The Complete Clerihews of E. Clerihew Bentley*, Oxford University Press, 1982.

# CHAPTER FOUR
## WRITING FREE VERSE POEMS

AS I MENTIONED EARLIER, THERE ARE NO STEP-BY-STEP directions for writing a good poem. There are certain things that happen in a good poem, of course, but they may fall into place at different times during the writing process. What you want to say and how you want to say it may come easily in one poem, but your next poem may be more difficult to complete. You may decide that an image you thought was clear is really muddled. Or, after you've written a number of drafts and tinkered with the poem for a while, new words may come to mind.

A good poem is original. It uses clear language to say something in a compelling way. The American poet Robert Francis said that a poem is like an arrow; it should wound the reader. He meant that a good poem should touch the reader (as well as the writer). That can happen in a number of ways. A poem might scare or anger him. Or, a poem might get a snicker or a belly laugh. A poem can touch like a hand on her shoulder in troubled times. Maybe it will bring a tear to her eye. Perhaps the poem will surprise the reader with a good ending.

But at the heart of every good poem, every poem that touches a reader, is the language. And don't worry if you think you can't be a poet because you don't have a good vocabulary. More often than not, the language of a poem is simple, ordinary language that the poet uses in inventive ways. When the right words combine, they frequently make meanings beyond the words themselves.

And it's all done with words. No high-tech special effects. No computer-enhanced remastered sound. No trick photography. Words. Those things we've used since we were babies. And when you sit down to write a poem, you have the power of the words at your fingertips. If you work at a poem, you can share your feelings with your readers. You can share how you see the world. And, if you write well, your readers will be touched by your gift.

In this section of the guide you will learn some of the basics of writing free verse poems. A free verse poem is a poem that is free of a set rhythm and rhyme. Among other things, I will talk about imagery, figurative language, rhythm, line breaks, and word choice. You will have a chance to write four types of poems: a list poem, a poem of address, a persona poem, and a narrative poem. Learning these types of poems will give you the tools to write about many of the topics and situations that interest you.

This seems like a good time to say something about the model poems I've included. Remember that the poems I've used as examples are like this book. They are meant to be guides, not blueprints. If your poem doesn't "fit" the model, that's fine.

Write *your* poem and don't worry about how close it is to the poem you are using as your model. I encourage you to experiment. Use what works for you and ignore what doesn't seem right for you. The more poems you write, the more confident you will be about taking chances. And when you do that, you will surprise yourself with the energetic and original poems you will write.

## LIST POEMS

The list poem is a great place to start when you want to write free verse poems. Although it looks easy to write, writing a truly good list poem takes more effort than simply jotting down a list. When we hear the word *list* we probably think of a column of words on a sheet of paper, like a shopping list or a list of your favorite movies or foods. Well, some list poems are like that. Here's one by Anne Waldman:

## Things That Go Away
## & Come Back Again

Thoughts
Airplanes
Boats
Trains
People
Dreams
Animals
Songs
Husbands
Boomerangs
Lightning
The sun, the moon, the stars
Bad weather
The seasons
Soldiers
Good luck
Health
Depression
Joy
Laundry

ANNE WALDMAN

But not all list poems have (mostly) one-word lines like Waldman's poem. Walt Whitman broke many of the rules of established poetry late in the nineteenth century when he wrote sprawling free verse poems in his magnificent book, *Leaves of*

*Grass*. Read aloud these opening lines from "I Hear America Singing," and you will hear the poem's music:

> I hear America singing, the varied carols I hear,
> Those of mechanics, each one singing his as it should
>     be blithe and strong,
> The carpenter singing his as he measures his plank or
>     beam,
> The mason singing his as he makes ready for work, or
>     leaves off work,
> The boatman singing what belongs to him in his boat,
>     the deckhand singing on the steamboat deck,
> The shoemaker singing as he sits on his bench, the
>     hatter singing as he stands,
> The wood-cutter's song, the ploughboy's on his way in
>     the morning, or at noon intermission or at sundown,
> The delicious singing of the mother, or of the young
>     wife at work, or of the girl sewing or washing,
> Each singing what belongs to him or her and to none
>     else,
> The day what belongs to the day—at night the party of
>     young fellows, robust, friendly,
> Singing with open mouths their strong melodious songs.
> WALT WHITMAN

Your list poems will very likely fall in between these extremes, perhaps like this poem:

## A History of Pets

Butch, black cocker spaniel, collected
stinks, dirt, and open wounds into which our
father poured gentian violet. Did not
come back one morning. A brown and white mutt
—I don't recall its name—was shot by our
mother, beheaded, and pronounced rabid
by health folks who provided all five of us
with fourteen Friday nights of shots. There was
Hooker, half-Persian cat who'd claw your back-
side through the open backed kitchen chairs and swing
by his hooks till you pulled him loose. Short-Circuit,
affectionate cat that walked crooked, that'd been
BB-shot in the head. Goat. Skunk. Some snakes.

DAVID HUDDLE

You may have noticed one thing these list poems have in common. They all describe or name things. Waldman names things and feelings. Whitman describes the "songs" of Americans. Huddle describes pets. (You might also notice that by naming and describing the pets he grew up with, Huddle gives us a good idea of how chaotic it must have been living in his home!)

I hope you see how these poets, particularly Whitman and Huddle, included specific details in their poems. Whitman writes about the carpenter "singing as he measures his plank or beam" and about the shoemaker "singing as he sits on his bench." And Hooker, one of Huddle's pets, was a "half-Persian cat who'd claw your back-/side through the open backed kitchen chairs and swing/by his hooks till you pulled him loose." It is rich details like these that make a poem, list poem or otherwise, come alive.

**Try This . . .** One type of list poem is a history poem, which details a part of the writer's life. If you've moved a lot, you might consider writing a history of the houses you've lived in or the schools you've attended. If you've been to summer camp, you could list some of the new things you tried. When you come up with some ideas, make sure you write them down in your journal before you forget them. Then, using Huddle's poem as a model, try your own history poem.

◆　◆　◆

Here's a poem written by a student as a variation on Huddle's poem:

A HISTORY OF THE FAULTY SHOES
Tiny white lacy slippers
   that I kicked off when I was a baby
Sweet little pink jellies
   that I wore on the swing set and broke the strap
Soft leather moccasins
   that had beads that fell off

Bright pink sneakers
 that were hard to lace up
Little purple velcro tennis shoes
 that had a hole in the heel
Shiny black party shoes
 that got scratched on the sidewalk
White leather sandals
 that got wet in the sprinkler and shrank
Green All-Stars
 that rubbed at the toe
Black Mary-Janes
 that I still wear today
But who knows?

AMANDA GRANUM

Another type of list poem you can write is the "how-to" poem. The boy who wrote the next list poem built it on things he says to get out of doing his homework:

### HOW TO GET OUT OF HOMEWORK

I'm feeling sick
Look at what the dog's doing
Five more minutes
That's a beautiful necklace
Oh, just a little longer
But, I just reached dark castle and I can't stop now
There's a bomb in my bedroom

There's a killer outside
The baby's sick
But this book is stretching my mind in ways
    homework can't
I'm feeling sleepy
I might wake the baby
I just heard a gunshot
Was that the phone?
After dinner?
The cat's outside
So is the dog
I'm hungry
I don't feel like it.

JARED CONRAD-BRADSHAW

While this poet used excuses to build his poem, you can also write a poem that is a set of directions, and you know how important clear directions are when you are trying something new.

Try This . . . In your journal make a list of subjects that might make an interesting how-to poem. Include things that are fairly simple. "How to Build a Car" would be too complicated. Something like "How to Make the Perfect Pizza" or "How to Be a Best Friend" might be more suitable. But you can also write zany how-to poems. For example, "How to Be a

Gerbil" or "How to Make a Rainbow" might make interesting poems.

Once you've made a list, pick the subject that interests you the most and begin drafting your how-to poem. Remember to include the words that will best help readers follow your directions.

◆   ◆   ◆

The history poem and the how-to poem are only two types of list poems. To get an idea of other kinds of list poems, take a look at this list of list poem subjects that was generated by a class of young writers I worked with:

| | |
|---|---|
| Things that never die | Things that come in handy |
| Things that annoy me | Things that are quiet |
| Achievements | Things I like about my friends |
| Things that stink | Memories I'd forgotten |
| Things that are gross | Make-believe places |
| Siblings | The perfect friend |
| My grandmother's house | What to do in study hall |
| Bad cooks | Nighttime |
| Irritating sounds | Lies I've told |
| What money can do | Embarrassing moments |
| Things I can't do & why | My mistakes |
| What cats do | What my teachers do at home |
| Lucky things | Attic |
| What to do if … | When I'm alone I … |

📖 Try This . . . Pick a topic from this list and begin drafting your list poem. Remember that these topics are suggestions, so feel free to change them to work for you.

◆    ◆    ◆

Here's a list poem by a young poet who uses one of the topics as a title and starting line:

> "WHEN I'M ALONE I . . ."
> think about my life
> it's gone up in smoke
> cry
> listen to my cat
> hear music play
> hold my breath
> scream
> sleep
> never dream
> sing along
> clean
> sneak a puff
> hold my breath
> watch the news
> have some coffee
> fix a meal
> do the dishes

sweep the floor
strum my guitar
mess up and start again

OLLIE DODGE

    I said earlier that writing a good list poem was more difficult than merely writing a list. But that is how you start, by writing a list of anything you can think of that's related to your subject. For example, suppose you want to write a poem called "Things That Drive Me Crazy." The first step is simple: Brainstorm a list of things that drive you crazy. Don't censor yourself. Don't listen to the voice that might be telling you, "This poem will never work," or "What a lame idea that is!" Write down whatever comes to mind. Take your time with your list. You might think you are finished, but if you let the list rest for a few days, you will more than likely come up with other items to add to it.

    When you have a good, long list, read it over carefully. Can you see some things on the list that are related to other things? You might realize, for example, that half of the items on your list of things that drive you crazy are about your younger brother. Great! That should tell you that your poem wants to be "Things About My Brother That Drive Me Crazy." Copy those things on a new page of your journal and let them be the basis for your poem.

    As you look at your list for your new poem, you may think of other things to add. Maybe you repeat some things that can be crossed out of your draft. Be careful to include in your poem only those things that give the reader a clear picture of how your brother annoys you.

When you think you have all the things that you want to include in your poem, examine the order in which they appear. Do you have a reason for putting things where you do? You should. You might want to start off your poem with little annoying things and work your way up to the more important ways in which your brother bugs you. Or, you might want to list the aggravating things he does in a "typical" day, starting with things he does or says in the morning and ending with what he does or says in the evening.

As you work on the draft of your list poem, read it out loud. How does it sound? Have you placed words together that start with the same consonant? Perhaps some words have the same vowel sounds. (You can read more about the sounds of words in POETCRAFT: SOUND on page 21.) What sort of rhythm does your poem have? Short lines will give it a more hurried feel than long lines. Does the rhythm fit with the subject of the poem? If you are writing about the joys of running on the cross-country track team, you might want to create a smooth rhythm to match the rhythm of distance running.

WRITING TIP FROM A POET

One way to deal with writer's block is to write free, to daydream in writing. When you write quickly, recklessly, there's often something uncovered you previously didn't know about. Another way is by reading. What others have written well can also open us up in unexpected ways.

Mark Vinz

## SOMETHING TO READ

In *Near the Window Tree* (Harper & Row, 1975), Karla Kuskin offers a generous selection of poems (and illustrations) as well as some prose anecdotes and suggestions for writers.

# POETCRAFT: WORD CHOICE

A basic skill that good poets must master is word choice. The poet's job is to find the best words for each line of the poem that she is working on. Rarely will a poet settle for the first words that hit the page. Sometimes finding the right word might involve using the thesaurus. It might mean trying different words and listening to how they affect the poem. Or, it might mean just letting the right word come to you while the poem sits in your drawer. As Mark Twain said, the difference between the right word and the almost right word is like the difference between lightning and a lightning bug. So, don't settle for a good word when a little work and thought will give you the right word.

With my first draft of "Bingo," I was interested in getting my ideas down on the paper. Who would be in the poem? What would they do? What story did I want the poem to tell? At this brainstorming part of the writing process, I wasn't overly concerned with word choice. I knew that I could find the right words as the poem worked its way through many drafts. I focused on finding vivid and expressive words, sometimes even surprising words.

### Bingo

Saturday night
Dad washed, I dried
the supper dishes
while Mom armed herself
for Early Bird bingo at seven
in the church basement:
her lucky piece
(a smooth quarter she'd won the first time out),
seat cushion,
and a White Owls box of pink plastic markers.

Dad read the paper
watched TV with me
until Mom returned,
announcing her triumph with a door slam
and a shout
"I was hot!"

Flinging her hat,
twirling out of her jacket,
she pulled dollar bills
from her pockets
before setting them free
to flutter like fat spring snow.

"Ninety-two dollars!" she squealed
as Dad hugged her off the floor.
"Ninety-two dollars!"

In bed I listened to
mumbled voices
planning to spend the money—
on groceries
school clothes
a leaky radiator—
and wished she'd buy
a shiny red dress
long white gloves
and clickety-click high heels.

Notice in the opening stanza that I used *armed* instead of *prepared*, because I wanted to suggest in a single word how seriously the mother takes her bingo. She gathers things as though readying herself for battle. Also, I was very specific about what she took with her.

In the third stanza, I changed *dropping* to *flinging* because I think it shows her exuberant attitude, and I added *twirling* to heighten that feeling. And when I wrote "setting them free/ to flutter like fat spring snow" (notice the repetition of the *f* sound), I wanted the reader to see the bills falling in slow motion.

I ended the poem with specific items that I hoped would emphasize the contrast between how the parents planned to spend the winnings—"on groceries/school clothes/a leaky radiator"—and what the young narrator wished his mother would buy with the money: "a shiny red dress/long white gloves/clickety-click high heels."

Even though most of the details in this poem are made up, I hoped that choosing the right words would make the scene come alive. Choosing the right words for your poem takes time and work, but it lets you speak from your heart about your subject.

**Try This** . . . Choose a draft of a poem that you haven't looked at for a while. Read through the poem, looking for words that do not quite create the image you were trying for. Look in the thesaurus for words that would work better. After you substitute strong, vivid words for weak, vague words re-write the poem and read it to a friend to get his reaction to the changes you've made. Are you more satisfied with the new version? Can you see other changes that would improve the poem?

◆　　◆　　◆

## POEMS OF ADDRESS

A poem of address is a poem that is written *to* somebody or *to* something. Although the reader will learn about the object or person that is the subject of the poem, a poem of address is not *about* that person or thing. That's an important point to keep in mind as you work on this poem. If you don't stay focused on writing a poem of address, it could easily turn into simply another poem about the subject.

When you start thinking of a subject, you might want to consider writing a poem to a person with whom you have some unfinished business. Perhaps your best friend has moved away or a treasured relative has died, and you never had a chance to tell her how much she meant to you. Or, perhaps you admire your father or one of your teachers. A poem of address is a good way to express those feelings.

A poem of address that deals with such unfinished business is:

### GRANDMOTHER

O Yaya, I miss you.
I know I never enjoyed
our Sunday lunches with you
inside the dining room
not out in the sun.
You were old
I was young.
I never talked to you
unless I was forced
but I didn't know
how much I loved you.
Now you are gone
I miss our lunches,
the dining room is empty,
the chairs pushed in tight.
And the maid has left.
So have you
and I wish you'd come back
because I miss you.

KATE MANTHOS

Of course, there are lots of other reasons for writing a poem
of address. Perhaps you're angry at the neighbor's dog who
always starts barking on a Saturday morning when you have a
chance to sleep in. You could also write to a friend who let you
down or to people who pollute our rivers and air. You could also
write a poem of address out of thanks. Maybe your big sister

gives you a ride to the mall every now and then. Maybe your mother tries to understand without prying when something is bothering you. Or, you might address your poem to the assistant principal who believes your excuses for being late to school ...most of the time.

One of the neat things about a poem of address is that you can write one to have fun. You can write one to your favorite character in a book, TV show, or computer game. You can write one to the person who invented your favorite food (like chocolate, pizza, or frozen waffles). Maybe you want to write a poem to the snow that caused school to be called off the Friday your not-quite-finished research project was due.

**Try This** . . . You can also write a poem of address to an object. Such as to your armpits because they always seem to sweat at the wrong times. You could write a poem to one of our modern conveniences like the microwave oven, the computer, the VCR, or the compact disc player. Look around. There are lots of objects that you could write a poem to.

◆    ◆    ◆

SOMETHING TO READ

In *Neighborhood Odes* (Scholastic, 1994) Gary Soto writes odes (poems of celebration and admiration) about a sprinkler, fireworks, weight lifting, family photographs, and *la tortilla*.

Another book of celebratory poems by Soto is *Canto Familiar* (Harcourt Brace, 1995).

When you think you have a suitable topic, quickly jot down the reasons why you want to write a poem to this person or thing. Be specific. That list will likely wind up being the backbone of your poem. If you're angry, try to list the reasons why. If you're writing out of admiration, try to capture your feelings about your subject. Why do you admire it? If you are writing a poem on a fun subject, don't forget to be playful. You still need to be specific, but in a playful poem there is room for exaggeration, overstatement, and downright goofiness, as in this poem:

### Hiccups

Dear Hiccups,
You're the enemy of my mouth and throat.
You're the worst thing that could ever — hic — happen!
If you ever should disturb me again,
I shall toss you out of my vocal chords.
You're like hail on an angry alligator.
So, catch my drift, dear hiccups — hic —
and get far, far away.
Get out — hic — DEAR, AWFUL HICCUPS!
— hic —

Jennifer Nussinow

# POETCRAFT: FIGURATIVE LANGUAGE

A good way to describe something—such as a person, a place, or a feeling—is to compare it to something else. We do this all the time in our conversation when we say things like, "She's as light as a feather" or "My brother is a pig." Although these comparisons are not very original, notice that they compare things that are dissimilar—a girl and a feather, a boy and a pig—and both create images that appeal to the senses. A feather is something we can see and feel, while we can see, hear, touch, and smell a pig.

You can make your writing come alive by using vivid, original comparisons. When you compare something to something else, you are using a metaphor. When you make a comparison that uses "like" or "as," that is a simile. Usually, a metaphor will be more of an attention grabber than a simile in your poem. A simile is more mild mannered. For example, notice the way I used metaphors in this poem:

REVEREND MONA

When the elders said she was too old,
Reverend Mona
surrendered her tabernacle
next to Fast Frankie's Pawn Shop
and dropped out of sight

long enough for people to wonder.
She returned,
a shaggy boat
leading a wake of dogs —
shepherd,
Husky,
mutts —
to preach on a bench
near a crescent of marigolds,
while her hounds sat,
a congregation in restless prayer.

I walked away
before our eyes could meet.

You can see how I compare Reverend Mona to a boat "leading a wake of dogs" and call her dogs "a congregation in restless prayer." Both metaphors help give the reader a sharp picture of this woman and her pack of dogs. Both comparisons would have been weaker, I think, if I had put in a "like" or an "as" and written them as similes.

Here is a checklist of a few questions to answer as you try to come up with fresh metaphors:

✓ How would you describe that object or place?

✓ How does it make you feel?

✓ What does it remind you of?

✓ What object, emotion, or experience could you compare it to?

**Try This** . . . In your journal, write metaphors for these things:

a swiftly flowing river

a calm, blue lake

a snake coiled on a rock

a long, dark hallway

a partially torn basketball net

◆ ◆ ◆

Although metaphors may sound stronger than similes, similes are still a wonderful way to create vivid images in your poems. Here are a few of the similes I've used:

- eyes as dark as a night river
- with cuffs stiff
  as the ace of spades
- hands as tough and smooth
  as the underside of a tortoise
- as graceful as a coatrack
- perched on counter stools
  like gulls on a pier

As you work on your metaphors and similes, you will learn

how to skillfully make them a part of your poems. One thing to keep in mind when you make a comparison is to be certain that your reader will understand the things you are comparing. If I tell you that my new jacket is "as brown as a Siberian mud snake," that wouldn't help you visualize the color of my jacket because you have never seen a Siberian mud snake. (I know because I just made it up!) However, if I tell you that my jacket is as brown as a new football, then you get a good idea of the color.

Good similes make your poems come alive because they link two things that aren't ordinarily thought of as being similar. This is what good writing is all about: letting the readers see things in new ways.

**Try This . . .** In your journal, write fresh comparisons for the following:

His eyes are like _____.

Her snowball throwing is like _____.

The trees are as tall as _____.

The sun was as hot as _____.

The (cold/hot) water felt like _____.

◆　◆　◆

Another type of figurative language is personification, which is when you give human qualities to inanimate objects. For example, we might say, "The wind howled through the night," or "The old house groaned in the fierce hurricane."

Notice how Elinor Wylie gives the sea murderous human qualities in her poem:

## Sea Lullaby

The old moon is tarnished
With smoke of the flood,
The dead leaves are varnished
With colour like blood,

A treacherous smiler
With teeth white as milk,
A savage beguiler
In sheathings of silk,

The sea creeps to pillage,
She leaps on her prey;
A child of the village
Was murdered today.

She came up to greet him
In a smooth golden cloak,
She choked him and beat him
To death, for a joke.

Her bright locks were tangled,
She shouted for joy,

With one hand she strangled
A strong little boy.

Now in silence she lingers
Beside him all night
To wash her long fingers
In silvery light.

ELINOR WYLIE

Here are some suggestions of ways to include personification in your poems:

You can use a verb that shows human actions.

*Rain danced on the deserted street.*

You can use personal pronouns to refer to objects.

*The stream glides on her way through the forest.*

You can refer to human body parts on inanimate objects.

*The oak lifted its mighty arms to the summer sun.*

**Try This . . .** Choose an object, such as a river or a car or an ice cube, and practice the different ways you can use personification to make that thing come alive. Use a fresh page in your journal so you have plenty of space to try out different possibilities. Here are two examples:

*The floor seemed to remember Uncle Waldo because it groaned when he walked across the room.*

*The creek slid swiftly between her rocky banks.*

◆ ◆ ◆

Figurative language is crucial to poetry. It connects large abstract ideas such as love, friendship, war, and peace to the physical world of the reader. Through figurative language the writer reveals and clarifies her ideas by evoking the senses and creating pictures in the reader's mind. Original use of figurative language offers the reader a unique view of the poem's subject, transforms an idea or experience into something memorable, allows language to work on more than one level, and helps distinguish poetry from other genres. So, collect objects, save old keys, broken calculators, seashells and driftwood, observe your environment carefully and explore how these physical "things" can stand for something beyond themselves.

Judith Steinbergh

## PERSONA POEMS

In a sense, the persona poem is the opposite of a poem of address. In a persona poem you *become* another person or object and write a poem from that point of view. Here is a persona poem written by Siv Cedering:

### MITTEN DREAMS
In the summer
we sleep

in the attic,
dreaming the mothballs
into snowballs,

dreaming the air cold
so your hands will want to hide
inside the soft white clouds
of mittens,
that would make your hands

feel
like paws of snow
leopards, paws of white
tigers, paws of polar
bears.

SIV CEDERING

I can imagine that a pair of mittens caught Cedering's eye one day, and she began wondering what the mittens might have to say if they could speak. I wouldn't be surprised if she then took some time to observe the mittens and think of them put away for the winter, jotting notes along the way when something struck her fancy. But, since she had no idea what mittens would think, she let her imagination kick into high gear and imagined herself to be the mittens. The result, after numerous revisions, I suspect, was "Mitten Dreams."

The persona poem is another chance for you to let your

observations and your imagination work hand in hand. Let yourself wonder about what you see around you, then let your imagination in on the fun. What might it be like to be your baby brother crawling along on the floor? Get down on all fours and check it out. The world looks quite different from down there! And while you're at it, observe him crying to get out of a playpen, sucking on his fist, or sitting in a high chair getting fed. What might he say at those times? What might he be thinking and feeling? Can you make such thoughts and feelings part of your poem?

You can write a persona poem that reflects your personality or your own feelings. If you feel unwanted and left out, for example, you might want to write a poem as a stray dog. If you feel unattractive or unappreciated, you can write a poem as an animal or a plant that is not considered appealing to the eye, like an ostrich or a dandelion. Here's a persona poem in which the young writer is a crocodile:

CROCODILE
I glide through the greeny depths
Like a slow log
An old moss covered log
I spot my prey
with just my keen eyes showing
I dive silently underwater
Swimming closer
I can see it through the water

I wait a few moments
For the perfect time to strike
Then I leap through the air
With the glare of blood in my eyes
I sink my teeth into my prey
And drag it down, down into the water
And twist it, turn it
Until it has drowned
And then I chomp on it
And swallow it down
Then I feel like it's time for a nap.

WILL CLAXTON

Try This . . . You can also write a persona poem from the point of view of a character in a fairy tale or a nursery rhyme. It's fun to pick a character that is not the main character. For instance, you could write a poem as one of Cinderella's stepsisters or as the Prince. Or, what was life like for the dish and the spoon after they ran away together? Or, what might Old King Cole have to say for himself?

◆   ◆   ◆

When you look for a subject, you might want to consider things that are near enough for you to easily observe. For example, you might want to consider writing a persona poem as wind chimes, a taillight, a tennis ball, a kitten, or a dented trash can. Before you can write a good persona poem, you need to understand your subject. What makes it what it is? For example, what makes a cat what it is? What makes it different as a pet from, say, a dog or a ferret? What might a cat think, want, fear? How can you put it all into words? That's your job as a poet. Here's what a young writer wrote after observing a pond near his home:

CALM POND

I am free to move
In summer, spring, and fall
The wind moving about me
The tiniest ripples
Moving end to end
People come to me
For their thinking place
It is calm and
I hear the slightest sound
A bird from the tallest tree
A frog swims swiftly
Through my black water
Then nestles in the soft mud
At the bottom
Tadpoles waiting for their big day

The days are getting colder
And colder each day
Now I am frozen
And I can't move
Like I used to

Now I wait patiently
For spring to come.

IAN PULLEN

When you've written some persona poems that you are satisfied with, you might try writing a dialogue poem or a poem that gives two sides of a story. What would Jack and Jill have to say about what went on while they were going up the hill? (Or about what went on after all the excitement died down?) What might your locker say to the locker next to it when nobody's around? Would it complain about the mess or the smell or the noise?

The more you look around and observe, the more subjects you will find for your persona poems. After you've written a few persona poems, your imagination will take over and let you see and hear things that will astound you. But you must be ready. Be alert. Keep your eyes and ears open. And keep a notebook handy to capture all the surprising ideas that come your way.

---

WRITING TIP FROM A POET

Get in the habit of quietly observing and experiencing the world around you. Trust your five senses to lead you to ideas, which are everywhere, just waiting for you to connect with them—and make them your own.

Bobbi Katz

## Something to Read

*Advice for a Frog* (Lothrop, Lee and Shepard Books, 1995) by Alice Schertle is a dazzling collection in which the poet introduces us to a menagerie of remarkable creatures.

## Narrative Poems

A narrative poem is one that tells a story. You are probably familiar with some of the long narrative poems that tell stories of fictional characters, poems such as "The Cremation of Sam McGee" by Robert Service, or "Casey at the Bat" by Ernest Thayer. You might even recall the opening lines of "The Highwayman":

The wind was a torrent of darkness among the gusty trees.
The moon was a ghostly galleon tossed upon cloudy seas.
The road was a ribbon of moonlight over the purple moor,
And the highwayman came riding—
      Riding—riding—
The highwayman came riding, up to the old inn-door.

ALFRED NOYES

When you write a narrative poem, most likely the story will be about something that happened to you. The first place you can look for a subject for your story poem is in your journal. If you've been keeping a journal, you may have a rich treasure chest of memories to consider for your poem. And, if you are attentive to what is happening around you every day, you will notice new experiences that will be worth writing about. Just make sure that you save them in your journal. Writing a narrative poem gives you the chance to capture in words the significant incidents of your life as well as the feelings that go along with them. (Of course, you might want to invent a character and write a narrative poem about him or her, or continue the story of a character that already exists, like Casey after he made the final out in "Casey at the Bat.")

Since many of our memories are connected to objects, you might find a good subject if you look through that shoe box or the bottom drawer where you keep the souvenirs of your life. That seashell might recall last summer's visit to the ocean with your family. That woven bracelet was given to you by a new friend you met at camp. A brass doorknob reminds you of the apartment you used to live in. While you can certainly write a poem describing these objects, look beyond the object to the memory or story it brings to mind.

Bear in mind that not all your memories or stories will be pleasant. Some of our most vivid memories are unhappy ones. Family members die. Neighbors move away. Friendships end. We fail at things that are important to us. Those sorts of things happen to everyone. It's a good idea to write about these memories as well as the happy ones because it might help us understand these memories or learn how better to deal with them. Also, a reader may take comfort in your poem when she recalls that the same thing happened to her. In this way, poetry can connect us to one another and offer consolation.

When you write about memories it is important to keep one thing in mind: You do not need to stick to the facts. You are writing poetry, not history, so it is all right to change some details to make your poem more dramatic or more entertaining. When we read "Cottontail" by George Bogin, we have no idea if this memory is factually accurate. That doesn't matter. The important thing is that the poem rings true when we read it.

### COTTONTAIL

A couple of kids,
we went hunting for woodchucks
fifty years ago
in a farmer's field.
No woodchucks
but we cornered
a terrified
little cottontail rabbit
in the angle
of two stone fences.
He was sitting up,
front paws together,
supplicating,
trembling
while we were deciding
whether to shoot him
or spare him.
I shot first
but missed,
thank god.
Then my friend fired

and killed him
and burst into tears.
I did too.
A little cottontail.
A haunter.

GEORGE BOGIN

Suppose, for example, you want to write about the day your family pet of many years died. The incident is very vivid to you because it was such a sad day. You remember that the day was bright and sunny. However, it doesn't have to be a bright, sunny day in the poem you write about that event. You can have the day be cloudy or stormy because that adds to the mood or shows how you were feeling at the time. On the other hand, you might want to keep it a bright and sunny day because it makes a strong contrast to what you were going through. In either case, make sure you describe the day vividly. The point is worth remembering: You do not need to stick to the facts when you write your poems. Writing honestly has little to do with the facts, unless, of course, you are writing a poem that requires historical or scientific accuracy.

Try This . . . If you have trouble starting your narrative poem, you can always draft it as a prose story. Put in all the specific details, all the vivid language, all the honest feelings that will make the incident come alive. When you are satisfied that you've included what's important, read through your draft and draw a circle around every word and phrase that is absolutely essential to your story. (No fair drawing a big circle around the whole story!) It might be a word here, a phrase there. When you have drawn all your circles, copy all those words on a new sheet of paper, writing whatever was in a circle on a new line. In other words, if you circled a single word, it goes on one line of your next draft. If your next circle included several words, they go on the next line. And so on. When you have finished recopying all the encircled words, your draft will look like a poem. It isn't a poem, not yet, but it is beginning to resemble one. Now you are ready for the real work of writing: revising.

Read over what you have written. Does it make sense? Not completely. You will need to add some connecting words—but be careful to add only what's absolutely essential. You will need to cut out and change other words. Slowly, as you repeat this process, your poem will emerge. It will take time and focus, of course, but from your original mass of words will come a poem that tells your story as only you can tell it.

❖   ❖   ❖

Since setting, or place, might be important in your narrative poem, be sure to include details that appeal to your senses: sight, sound, smell, taste, and touch. I don't mean that every scene must include every sense, but make sure you include the senses that are especially important to the scene you are describing. For example, if your poem is set in your grand-mother's house, you might want to include details that appeal to the sense of smell. But don't be satisfied with saying, "I recall how wonderful my grandmother's house smelled." That's vague. It doesn't create a word picture. Instead write something like, "When I think of my grandmother's house, I remember the smell of baking bread and frying chicken." Can you see how these details would give your reader a better sense of what it was like in your grandmother's house?

A good way to describe something is to use figurative language and to make comparisons. Metaphors, similes, and personification are a few ways a writer can make a scene or feeling come alive. If you're not sure how these types of figurative language work, the POETCRAFT: FIGURATIVE LANGUAGE (page 63) should help you.

---

WRITING TIP FROM A POET

If you are troubled or sad or lonely, pick up your pencil and tell the page about how you feel. Don't think. Just do it. Poems are made from what life gives us, good or bad. You will be surprised by what happens. You will probably have written a poem. Try it. Be a poet.

Julia Cunningham

---

## SOMETHING TO READ

The exciting story of the world's most famous women pirates comes alive in Jane Yolen's narrative poem, *The Ballad of the Pirate Queens* (Harcourt Brace, 1995).

# POETCRAFT: LINE BREAKS

There are no rules about where a line ends in free verse. But that is no reason to panic, or to simply write a poem without giving any thought to where the lines break. Keep in mind that line break is often as important a part of a free verse poem as end rhyme is to a poem written in couplets.

Basically, when you write a free verse poem, you want to keep the words that belong together on the same line. This will mean that sometimes your line will end with punctuation, but more often it will probably run over onto the next line. There are a number of reasons—too many to list here—for breaking up lines in a particular way, but consider the reasons on this checklist:

✓ You may want to emphasize a word or phrase, so you would put it at the end of a line or on a line by itself.

✓ Carrying a word or phrase to the next line may add suspense or surprise to your poem.

✓ You might want to arrange your poem so the alignment of the lines creates a desired visual effect.

✓ Sometimes it just feels right to break lines in a certain way. Don't be afraid to follow your intuition in this way.

As I've said, when you draft a poem it's okay if you write it to look like a paragraph or a chunk of prose. After you do some tinkering with sharpening the images and the language, you can simply draw slash marks where you think the line breaks should come. Then copy your poem onto a new sheet of paper, making sure that you put in your line breaks. Your poem will not be finished at this point, of course, but it's starting to look like a poem, and you can now revise it further, perhaps even changing some of the line breaks.

**Try This . . .** I've taken one of my poems from *Brickyard Summer* and rewritten it as a prose passage. Read through it and see if you can get a sense of which words belong together on each line of the poem. On the next page I'll show you the poem as it appeared in the book. No peeking! Try this exercise *then* look at the poem.

"Raymond"

Hair the color of pencil shavings, eyes as dark as a night river, best friend since fifth grade when he seemed to stop growing. Large enough to blacken Danny Webb's eye when he said, "Hiya, pipsqueak," the first day of eighth grade, small enough to get into the movies as a kid. At the Top Hat Cafe, gave me one play on his juke box quarters. For three nights, trusted me with the false teeth (uppers only) he found on a park bench. In The Tattoo Emporium, let me help him pick out the eagle-holding-thunderbolt he'd claim for his chest the day he turned eighteen.

### RAYMOND

Hair the color of pencil shavings,
eyes as dark as a night river,
best friend
since fifth grade
when he seemed to stop
growing.

Large enough
to blacken Danny Webb's eye
when he said,
"Hiya, pipsqueak,"
the first day of eighth grade,

small enough
to get into the movies as a kid.

At the Top Hat Cafe,
gave me one play
on his juke box quarters.

For three nights,
trusted me
with the false teeth
(uppers only)
he found on a park bench.

In The Tattoo Emporium,
let me help him
pick out the
eagle-holding-thunderbolt
he'd claim for his chest
the day he turned eighteen.

Chances are you came pretty close to breaking the lines the way I did. Probably not exactly, but that's okay. We have all read poems in which the line breaks seem arbitrary. In fact, if I were to tinker with "Raymond," I could find a few line breaks that I would change. For example, in the last stanza, I would leave "pick out" on that line and move "the" to the next line to go with "eagle-holding-thunderbolt." The important thing to keep in mind is that as a poet you must have your reasons for putting certain words on certain lines in your poem. So, make sure when you revise, you pay attention to line breaks. One good way to do that is to read the poem carefully aloud because you will hear things you might miss when you read the poem silently.

◆ ◆ ◆

Finally, let me offer one more checklist you might want to use when you write a poem:

✓ Choose a topic for your poem that interests you. If you are not interested in it, there's no way you can expect your reader to be interested in it.

✓ Take the time to brainstorm freely some ideas related to the topic. See what happens.

✓ Don't settle for using "good" words in your poem. Work until you get the *right* word.

✓ Read your poem aloud, to yourself or to someone else.

✓ Find someone who will read your poem carefully and offer suggestions.

✓ Let your poem rest out of sight for a while before you look at it again.

✓ Remember: Revision means to see again. Revise with care.

Learning to write a good poem is like learning to play the piano or turn a double play. It takes practice and patience. Don't be discouraged if your early poems don't say exactly what you want them to say. The more you work at the craft of writing a poem, the more your poems will shine like diamonds. Look and listen to life with care. Practice your writing. Give yourself time to be a better poet. You will be pleased with what writing poetry can bring to your life.

# CHAPTER FIVE
## WHEN YOUR POEM IS FINISHED

YOU SHOULD WRITE POEMS FOR YOURSELF. BECAUSE YOU want to. Or, better, because you *have* to write poems to express the emotions you're feeling or to examine the way you see things. If you truly write for yourself, you'll be happy saving your poems in a fat folder or binder as you work harder to make better poems. You will know the satisfaction of shaping words into an engaging poem.

## MAKING BOOKS

On the other hand, you might feel that you want other people to read your poems. If you have a number of poems ready to publish, you can consider putting them into a book. When you think of a book of poems, you probably think of the traditional kinds of books we are all used to reading. And that certainly is one way to publish your poems. But there are easy ways to make less formal books. The easiest way to make a book is to fold sheets of paper down the center and staple them together along the center fold. You can then print your poems or, if you have the talent, write them in calligraphy on the blank pages.

For a more professional-looking book, you can use a word-processing program to print your poems. Check the computers at your school. There is probably a word-processing or desktop publishing program installed on the hard drives. These programs allow you to select a type face and printing arrangement which will work best for your poems.

To dress up your book you might want to use a sheet of colored paper for the cover. For a firmer cover, you could use poster board or a file folder.

While a stapled booklet works quite well, a booklet that is stitched together looks even better. You will need some basic equipment and patience to create a nicely sewn book, but there are a number of helpful books that you might find in your library. For starters, you can look for these:

*Book Craft*, Henry Pluckrose, Franklin Watts, 1992.

*Making Cards*, Charlotte Stowell, Larousse Kingfisher Chambers, 1995.

*Making Shaped Books*, Gillian Chapman and Pam Robson, The Millbrook Press, 1997.

*Making Shaped Books with Patterns*, Gillian Chapman and Pam Robson, The Millbrook Press, 1995.

*The Young Author's Do-It-Yourself Book: How to Write, Illustrate, & Produce Your Own Book*, Donna Guthrie, Nancy Bentley, and Katy Keck Arnsteen, The Millbrook Press, 1994.

Another type of book that you can make is a concertina or accordion book, which looks just like its name implies. If you have ever folded a piece of paper so it looks like an accordion, you have the basic idea of this type of book. One of the good things about it is that it requires no equipment or supplies to hold it together. Check *Making Shaped Books* for more help with the concertina book. You can have a lot of fun with it.

## MAKING CARDS AND POSTERS

One of my favorite ways of sharing new poems is to print them on bright-colored cards and mail them to friends and family. Nothing fancy, just the black letters on an orange or yellow postcard. If you feel more adventuresome—and have more talent for drawing than I do!—you can include your poem in a folded card that opens like a regular greeting card. Paint a picture on the front, and you have a thoughtful gift to send to someone special. (If you put your artwork on the inside of the card facing the poem, you can tape the card shut and write the address on one of the blank sides.) Another possibility is to use a photograph instead of artwork. Or, you can make a pop-up card, something I learned recently with my daughter. A few cuts and a fold or two, and your card will come alive in the reader's hands. *Making Cards* will be very helpful if you want to take a crack at a pop-up card.

What if your poem is too long to fit on one card? You could divide the poem into parts and send "installments," say, once a week until you've sent the whole poem. Or, you could make a poster that can be rolled up or folded for presentation.

And don't forget that you can put your poem on a poster and jazz it up with a painting or a drawing or pictures cut from a magazine. A poster can be simply a sheet of typing paper, or it can be larger, like a piece of oak tag. The bigger the poster, the more room you have for your art and the larger you can write your poem. On the other hand, sometimes bigger isn't better, especially if your poem is short.

If you've ever received a handmade gift, you probably remember the thrill of being blessed with a gift that someone special worked on just for you. Well, when you write a terrific poem and present it to someone on a card or poster, you are giving that person a gift he or she will cherish for a long time.

## SUBMITTING POEMS TO A PUBLISHER

Finally, let me say a few words about submitting your poems to a magazine or a contest. Most writers will admit that they like seeing their poems in a magazine or book because it means that many people have a chance to read their work. There are a number of magazines that publish poems written by students, and you might be interested in submitting some of your work to them. But, be warned: Lots of young writers are trying to do the very same thing with their poems, so it is very competitive. You must decide to submit nothing but your very best efforts.

Where should you submit your poems? First of all, check the magazines you like to see if they accept poetry submissions. If they do, you might want to start with those magazines. If they do not, then you need to do some research. Start in the periodicals room of your local library. Find the magazines for young readers and see if they accept poetry. Read some back issues to make sure that the kind of poems you write would be appropriate for a particular magazine. For examples, some magazines consider only free verse poems. Others may only publish poems about religious themes or nature or astronomy. Don't waste your time—and the editor's time—by submitting material that a magazine would not possibly publish.

If you want a wider selection of magazines for young readers, visit a good bookstore and see what they have on their racks. If you find some promising magazines, check to see if they will send you a sample copy and a set of their writers' guidelines. Most magazines will send both, although usually for a small fee. Build a file of magazines that publish the kind of poetry that you write. And submit your poems to those magazines.

Get a copy of *Market Guide for Young Writers* by Kathy Henderson (Writer's Digest Books, 1996). It's a terrific resource if you want to submit poems for publication. A good library will have a copy, although if you are serious about submitting poems, you might want to invest in your own copy.

Once you decide where you want to submit your poems, you need to make sure that you improve your chances of having a poem accepted by following the rules for submitting poems. As I said earlier, you should send only your best poems. Make sure that you correct all grammar, punctuation, and spelling mistakes in your poem before you mail it to a magazine.

There are some special considerations if you plan to submit your poems to a contest. Each contest has its own specific guidelines and rules that you must follow. So, when you learn of a contest, send for the guidelines and make sure you follow them. Some contests may require you to pay a small fee, so make sure you are prepared to do that. A number of contests publish the winning poems in a magazine or book. If possible, you should read the winning entries to see what kinds of poems have won in the past.

Many, many writers have poems rejected by magazines and contests. But I'd suggest that you not judge the quality of your work by the opinion of a magazine editor or contest judge. Your poem is as good as you've made it, regardless of what someone else thinks about it. I know young writers who wanted so badly to have their poem published that they began to write for magazines and contests instead of writing for themselves. Don't let that happen to you. Write your poems for you. Share them with family and friends, if you like. Submit them to contests and magazines, if you like. But always remember that *you* are the one who has to be satisfied with your poems. True, you need to work to make your poems better, but if you like a poem, then the poem is successful. You have every right to be pleased and proud of your work.

# A CHECKLIST OF GOOD POETRY BOOKS

*Advice for a Frog.* Alice Schertle. Lothrop, Lee, and Shepard, 1995.

*All the Small Poems and Fourteen More*. Valerie Worth. Farrar, Straus & Giroux, 1994.

*American Sports Poems*. Compiled by R.R. Knudson and May Swenson. Orchard Books, 1988.

*The Ballad of the Pirate Queens*. Jane Yolen. Harcourt Brace, 1995.

*Been to Yesterdays: Poems of a Life*. Lee Bennett Hopkins. Boyds Mills Press, 1994.

*Brats*. X.J. Kennedy. McElderry Books, 1986.

*Brown Angels: An Album of Pictures and Verse*. Walter Dean Myers. HarperCollins, 1993.

*Canto Familiar*. Gary Soto. Harcourt Brace, 1995.

*Caribbean Dozen: Poems From Caribbean Poets*. Edited by John Agard and Grace Nichols. Candlewick, 1994.

*Celebrate America: In Poetry and Art*. Edited by Nora Panzer, illustrated with works of art from the National Museum of American Art, Smithsonian Institution. Hyperion, 1994.

*Classic Poems to Read Aloud*. Compiled by James Berry. Kingfisher, 1995.

*Cool Salsa: Bilingual Poems on Growing Up Latino in the United States*. Edited by Lori M. Carlson. Holt, 1994.

*Could We Be Friends?: and Other Poems for Pals*. Bobbi Katz. Mondo, 1996.

*Dance With Me*. Barbara Juster Esbensen. HarperCollins, 1995.

*The Dragons Are Singing Tonight*. Jack Prelutsky. Greenwillow, 1993.

*The Dream Keeper: and Other Poems*. Langston Hughes. Knopf, 1994.

*The Earth Under Sky Bear's Feet: Native American Poems of the Land*. Joseph Bruchac. Philomel, 1995.

*I Feel a Little Jumpy Around You: A Book of Her and His Poems Collected in Pairs*. Edited by Naomi Shihab Nye and Paul B. Janeczko. Simon & Schuster, 1996.

*The Inner City Mother Goose*. Eve Merriam. Simon & Schuster, 1996.

*The Invisible Ladder: A Young Readers' Anthology of Contemporary Poetry*. Selected by Liz Rosenberg. Holt, 1996.

*Joyful Noise: Poems for Two Voices*. Paul Fleischman. Harper-Collins, 1988.

*Life Doesn't Frighten Me*. Maya Angelou, illustrated by Jean-Michel Basquiat. Stewart, Tabori & Chang, 1993.

*Mummy Took Cooking Lessons and Other Poems*. John Ciardi. Houghton Mifflin, 1990.

*Near the Window Tree: Poems & Notes*. Karla Kuskin. Harper & Row, 1975.

*One at a Time*. David McCord. Little, Brown, 1977.

*The Place My Words are Looking For: What Poets Say About & Through Their Work*. Edited by Paul B. Janeczko. Bradbury Press, 1990.

*Poetspeak: In Their Work, About Their Work*. Selected by Paul B. Janeczko. Bradbury Press, 1983.

*Random House Book of Poetry for Children*. Selected by Jack Prelutsky. Random House, 1983.

*The Rattle Bag: An Anthology of Poetry*. Edited by Seamus Heaney and Ted Hughes. Faber & Faber, 1985.

*Reflections on a Gift of Watermelon Pickle...And Other Modern Verse*. Compiled by Stephen Dunning, Edward Lueders, Naomi Shihab Nye, Keith Gilyard, and Demetrice A. Worley. ScottForesman, 1995.

*Rich Lizard: And Other Poems*. Deborah Chandra. Farrar, Straus & Giroux, 1996

*Riddle•icious*. J. Patrick Lewis. Knopf, 1996.

*Sing a Song of Popcorn: Every Child's Book of Poems*. Selected by Beatrice Schenk de Regniers, Eva Moore, Mary Michaels White, and Jan Carr. Scholastic, 1988.

*Sing to the Sun*. Ashley Bryan. HarperCollins, 1992.

*The Space Between Our Footsteps: Poems and Paintings from the Middle East*. Naomi Shihab Nye. Simon & Schuster, 1998.

*A Suitcase of Seaweed and Other Poems*. Janet S. Wong. McElderry Books, 1996.

*Sweet Corn*. James Stevenson. Greenwillow, 1995.

*That Sweet Diamond: Baseball Poems*. Paul B. Janeczko. Atheneum, 1998.

*This Same Sky: A Collection of Poems From Around the World*. Selected by Naomi Shihab Nye. Simon & Schuster, 1992.

*A Time to Talk: Poems of Friendship*. Selected by Myra Cohn Livingston. McElderry Books, 1992.

*Turtle in July.* Marilyn Singer. Macmillan, 1989.

*Two-Legged, Four-Legged, No-Legged Rhymes.* J. Patrick Lewis. Knopf, 1991.

*Under All Silences: Shades of Love.* Selected by Ruth Gordon. Harper & Row, 1987.

*A Visit to William Blake's Inn: Poems for Innocent and Experienced Travelers.* Nancy Willard. Harcourt Brace, 1981.

*Waiting to Waltz: A Childhood.* Cynthia Rylant. Bradbury, 1984.

*Where the Sidewalk Ends: Poems and Drawings.* Shel Silverstein. HarperCollins, 1974.

# GLOSSARY

*(Terms marked with * are discussed in more detail in the text of this book. Terms in **bold** appear elsewhere in the glossary.)*

*ACROSTIC POEM: **free verse** poem in which the first letter of each line, when read downward, forms a word, usually the title and/or subject of the poem. For example:

> HARRY
> **H**appy
> **A**nd
> **R**arely
> **R**eady to
> **Y**ell.

*ALLITERATION: repetition of the initial consonants of words. For example, *Peter Pan*.

*ASSONANCE: repetition of the vowel sounds in words. For example, the *ee* sound in *meet me*.

*BALLAD: a **narrative**, rhyming poem or song characterized by short **stanzas** and simple words and usually telling a heroic and/or tragic story. Here are the first two stanzas of "John Henry," a traditional American ballad in ten stanzas:

> When John Henry was a little tiny baby
> Sitting on his mama's knee,

He picked up a hammer and a little piece of steel
Saying, "Hammer's going to be the death of me, Lord, Lord,
  Hammer's going to be the death of me."

John Henry was a man just six feet high,
Nearly two feet and a half across his breast.
He'd hammer with a nine-pound hammer all day
And never get tired and want to rest, Lord, Lord,
  And never get tired and want to rest.

And here are the opening stanzas from "Bonnie Barbara Allan," a traditional Scottish ballad:

It was in and about the Martinmas time,
  When the green leaves were afalling,
That Sir John Graeme, in the West Country,
  Fell in love with Barbara Allan.

He sent his men down through the town,
  To the place where she was dwelling;
"O hast and come to my master dear,
  If you be Barbara Allan."

[Martinmas is St. Martin's Day, November 11.]

BLANK VERSE: poetry written in unrhymed iambic pentameter (five iambic feet per line). Shakespeare's best plays are noted for their fine blank verse. Here's an example from *Romeo and Juliet*:

Give me my Romeo, and when he shall die,
Take him and cut him out in little stars,
And he will make the Face of Heav'n so fine
That all the World will be in love with Night
And pay no Worship to the garish Sun.

**CATALOG POEM:** another name for a **list poem**

**CINQUAIN:** a five-line poem of one or two sentences of twenty-two syllables divided in this way:

line 1: 2 syllables
line 2: 4 syllables
line 3: 6 syllables
line 4: 8 syllables
line 5: 2 syllables

Here is a cinquain by Adelaide Crapsey, who is believed to have "invented" this form in the early 1900s:

> NIAGRA
> How frail
> Above the bulk
> Of crashing water hangs,
> Autumnal, evanescent, wan,
> The moon.
>
> ADELAIDE CRAPSEY

**\*CLERIHEW:** a short rhyming poem written of two **couplets** that pokes gentle fun at a celebrity

**\*COUPLET:** two lines of poetry that rhyme. For example:

> Listen, my children, and you shall hear
> Of the midnight ride of Paul Revere

**ELEGY:** a lament, a poem of grief or mourning

**EPIC:** a very long, heroic **narrative poem** about a great and serious subject. Examples of epic poems include the *Iliad* and the *Odyssey*, as well as *Beowulf*, a long Old English poem.

**FEMININE RHYME:** a rhyme of two syllables, one stressed, one unstressed, e.g., *smother/another*

**\*FIGURATIVE LANGUAGE:** nonliteral expressions to get across certain ideas or things more vividly. **Metaphor**, **simile**, and **personification** are examples of figurative language.

**\*FREE VERSE:** a poem without predictable **rhyme**, **rhythm**, or length of line or **stanza.**

**HAIKU:** a form of poetry that developed in Japan. A haiku usually has seventeen syllables in three lines of five, seven, and five syllables. The poet tries to capture a simple scene from nature and to convey his/her strong feeling about it. The haiku should contain a seasonal word or suggest a season. Here are two classic Japanese haiku:

> An old silent pond . . .
> A frog jumps into the pond,
> splash! Silence again.
> > BASHŌ (1644–1694)

> Over the wintry
> forest, winds howl in a rage
> with no leaves to blow.
> > SOSEKI (1275–1351)

**\*HISTORY POEM:** a **list poem** that illustrates some sort of theme that runs through at least part of a poet's life

**\*HOW-TO POEM:** a **list poem** that gives directions or instructions

**HYPERBOLE:** excessive exaggeration to make a point in a poem. For example, Lady Macbeth uses hyperbole in Shakespeare's play, *Macbeth*, when she laments,

Here's the smell of blood still: all the
perfumes of Arabia will not sweeten this little hand.

*IMAGE: a picture the poet creates with vivid words that appeal to the reader's senses of sight, smell, sound, taste, and touch

LIMERICK: a type of light, humorous poem, generally nonsensical in nature, of five lines, in which lines 1, 2, and 5 rhyme, as do lines 3 and 4. The rhythm of a limerick is equally important. The lines that rhyme also have the same rhythm, as well as the same number of syllables. For example,

> A bridge engineer, Mister Crumpett,
> Built a bridge for the good River Bumpett.
> A mistake in the plan
> Left a gap in the span,
> But he said, "Well, they'll just have to jump it."

*LINE BREAK: where lines of poetry end

*LIST POEM: a poem that is based on a list or catalog of some sort created by the poet

LYRIC POEM: a poem that expresses the poet's observations and feelings and often tells of the poet's personal experiences

MASCULINE RHYME: a rhyme of one syllable, as in *click/stick*

*METAPHOR: a comparison of two dissimilar things that implies some sort of equality between the things, e.g., *My love is a blossoming flower.*

METER: the measured rhythm of a line of poetry, made of poetic units called feet, which are determined by the stressed and unstressed syllables in a word or phrase. (In the word *follow*, for example, the first syllable is stressed, the second is unstressed.) Four basic types of poetic feet are used: iamb, trochee, anapest, and dactyl. The chart below illustrates the stressed ( $\prime$ ) and unstressed ( $\smile$ ) syllables in each kind of foot and gives some examples:

| | | |
|---|---|---|
| $\smile\;\prime$ | iamb | surprise, today, apart, amaze, arrange |
| $\prime\;\smile$ | trochee | pretty, sunny, quarrel, water, buyer |
| $\smile\;\smile\;\prime$ | anapest | understand, disagree, introduce, intercede |
| $\prime\;\smile\;\smile$ | dactyl | elephant, syllable, carelessly, happily |

The number of feet in a line of poetry will determine how that line is described. A line with five feet of any kind in it, for example, is called pentameter. If those feet are iambs, the line is called iambic pentameter. Here are the names of the lines:

| FEET PER LINE | NAME |
|---|---|
| 1 | monometer |
| 2 | dimeter |
| 3 | trimeter |
| 4 | tetrameter |
| 5 | pentameter |
| 6 | hexameter |
| 7 | heptameter |
| 8 | octameter |

\*NARRATIVE POEM: a poem that tells a story

ODE: generally speaking, a poem that uses exalted language to celebrate a subject. Although classic odes followed a specific form and were written about formal subjects, such as solitude and a decorative Grecian urn, modern writers have written odes about more everyday subjects, such as watermelon and sneakers.

\*ONOMATOPOEIA: a word that makes the sound of the action it describes. For example, *bang*.

**\*OPPOSITE:** a short poem made up of *couplets* that describes something by describing its opposite

**PARODY:** an exaggerated, usually humorous, imitation. My "Ten Little Aliens" is a parody of the nursery rhyme "Ten Little Indians."

**\*PERSONA POEM:** a poem in which the poet writes from the point of view of another person or thing

**\*PERSONIFICATION:** a comparison that gives human qualities to inanimate objects, e.g., *The old house groaned in the fierce storm.*

**\*POEM OF ADDRESS:** a poem that is written *to* someone or *to* something

**POETIC LICENSE:** the imaginative freedom of poets to break some of the rules of standard English. For example, in writing a line in an acrostic poem that begins with *x*, you might use *xciting*, *xcellent*, or *xactly*.

**QUATRAIN:** a poem or **stanza** of four lines

**\*REFRAIN:** a line or lines repeated throughout a poem

**\*RHYME:** the repetition of sounds at the ends of words

**RHYME SCHEME:** the pattern of end rhymes in a poem, described with lowercase letters to indicate which lines rhyme. A limerick, for example, has a rhyme scheme of *aabba*, which means that the first, second, and fifth lines have the same rhyme, and the third and fourth lines have the same rhyme.

**\*RHYTHM:** the basic beat in a line of poetry, the sound pattern created by stressed and unstressed syllables (see METER)

**SENRYU:** a poem that follows the form of a haiku, but with a humorous slant. For example:

> O, unlucky man
> while eating shiny apple
> you find half a worm
> PAUL B. JANECZKO

*SIMILE: a comparison that uses "like" or "as," e.g., *He is as graceful as a coatrack*.

SONNET: a fourteen-line poem written in iambic pentameter that follows a particular rhyme scheme. The English, or Shakespearean, sonnet (three quatrains and a final couplet) has a rhyme scheme of *abab cdcd efef gg* while the Italian, or Petrarchan, sonnet (an eight-line octave of two quatrains, followed by a sestet) has a rhyme scheme of *abba cddc cfgefg*.

SPEAKER: a character telling a poem

*STANZA: a group of lines of poetry, usually similar in length and pattern. Among the most common stanza lengths are:

couplet: a two-line stanza
tercet: a three-line stanza
quatrain: a four-line stanza
quintet: a five-line stanza
sestet: a six-line stanza
septet: a seven-line stanza
octave: an eight-line stanza

SYMBOL: something in a poem, e.g., a person or an object, that stands for something larger than itself. For example, a poet might use an American flag as a symbol for freedom or patriotism, or a ring as a symbol of undying love.

\*SYNONYM POEM: a two-line rhyming descriptive poem with a first line composed of three or four synonyms

THEME: the underlying meaning of a poem, the idea it presents about people or about life. Although sometimes stated directly, the theme of a poem is more often suggested by the content of the poem. The theme reflects the poet's concerns or feelings about the subject.

# BIOGRAPHICAL NOTES

E(DMUND) C(LERIHEW) BENTLEY (1875–1956) is best known throughout the English-speaking world for his classic locked-room mystery novel, *Trent's Last Case* (Carroll and Graft, 1991). Bentley studied to become a lawyer, but chose a career as a journalist and, for many years, wrote for London newspapers. He published a few collections of light verse. *(p. 38)*

GEORGE BOGIN (1920–1988) spent much of his life in the retail furniture business and did not begin to write until he was in his late fifties. His poems appeared in a number of magazines. A generous selection of his poems can be found in his book, *In a Surf of Strangers* (University Presses of Florida, 1971). *(p. 77)*

SIV CEDERING lived the first 14 years of her life by the Arctic Circle in Sweden before she moved to America. She is the author of 17 books, including novels, children's books, and collections of poetry. She currently lives near the ocean on Long Island, New York, where she spends much of her time painting. *(pp. 37, 69)*

WILL CLAXTON was born in Dallas, Texas, but now lives in Maine, where he enjoys soccer, drawing, running track, and skiing with his family. He was a fifth grader when he wrote "Crocodile." *(p. 71)*

JARED CONRAD-BRADSHAW wrote "How to Get Out of Homework" when he was a seventh grader at the American School of London. He and his family have returned to the United States, and Jared now goes to school in Massachusetts. *(p. 49)*

ADELAIDE CRAPSEY (1878–1914) is remembered as the person who created the cinquain. Toward the end of her life and in failing health, she wrote a volume of poems, *Verse*. After her death, Adelaide Crapsey became an inspiration for young poets. *(p. 99)*

JULIA CUNNINGHAM has spent most of her life traveling and writing but she didn't publish her first piece of fiction until 1960, when she was forty-four years old. The *Vision of François the Fox* was inspired by a visit to France. Perhaps her most popular novel is *Dorp Dead* (Pantheon, 1965). *(p. 80)*

JIM DANIELS was born in Detroit in 1956. He is the author of ten collections of poetry, including, most recently, *Blessing the House* (University of Pittsburgh Press, 1997). He has also written a screenplay and a one-act play. He lives with his wife and their two children in Pittsburgh, where he teaches at Carnegie Mellon University. He is an avid cyclist and "a mediocre but enthusiastic" softball player. *(p. 4)*

OLLIE DODGE was a seventh grader in the Shenandoah Valley of Virginia when she wrote her list poem, "When I'm Alone I . . ." *(p. 52)*

AMANDA GRANUM was a seventh grader at the American School of London when she wrote "A History of the Faulty Shoes." She still lives in London and attends ASL. *(p. 48)*

CHRISTINE HEMP lives and writes on an old adobe ranch in Taos, New Mexico. She teaches poetry and writing workshops at schools, pueblos, colleges, science laboratories, and artist colonies across the United States and as far away as Britain and Tobago. A flute and guitar player, Christine believes that music colors her poems, as do her paintings. *(p. 12)*

DAVID HUDDLE has published poems, short stories, reviews, and essays. A professor of English at the University of Vermont and at the Bread Loaf School of English, Huddle believes that naps are "an essential part of a writing life." *(p. 47)*

BOBBI KATZ has written poetry, picture books, and articles for teachers and librarians. She has worked as a freelance writer, a social worker, executive director of a weekly radio program, and editor of environmental materials. Until her retirement a few years ago, she worked as an editor and in-house writer for a major publisher. *(p. 74)*

X.J. KENNEDY began his writing career when he was nine years old and published homemade comic books to sell to his friends for a nickel. Since then he has published poems for adults as well as poems for young readers. You might want to look for *Uncle Switch* (McElderry Books, 1997), a book of limericks. Kennedy, who has five grown children, lives with his wife in Massachusetts next to a busy bicycle path and a one-cow farm. *(p. 30)*

KARLA KUSKIN, a native New Yorker, began writing early in her childhood and received much encouragement from her parents. "As far back as I can remember," she says, "poetry has had a special place in my life." She has published many books of poetry, some of which—like *Dogs and Dragons, Trees and Dreams,* and *Soap Soup and Other Verses* (Demco, 1994)—she illustrated herself. *(p. 44)*

MYRA COHN LIVINGSTON (1926–1996) began writing poetry when she was a first-year college student, and published her first poem in 1946. She went on to create an enormous body of work that includes poetry anthologies and books of her own poems for children. She said that writing was hard work, a process of "growing, discarding, and keeping only the best." *(p. 10)*

GEORGE ELLA LYON was born in the mountains of Kentucky, the daughter of a dry-cleaner and a community worker. Her first ambition was to be a neon sign maker. In addition to poetry in magazines and anthologies, Lyon has published 3 novels and 17 picture books. She lives in Kentucky with her husband and two sons. *(p. 2)*

KATE MANTHOS was born in London where she still lives. She attends the American School of London. A seventh grader when she wrote "Grandmother" *(p. 60)*, Kate enjoys writing, listening to music, and traveling.

ALFRED NOYES (1880–1958) is best known in his native England, as well as in the United States, for his ballads and romantic narrative poems. However, he also published fiction and drama in his lifetime. Although he is perhaps best remembered for "The Highwayman," his historic imagination is also apparent in his earlier books of poems, such as *Tales of the Mermaid Tavern*. *(p. 75)*

JENNIFER NUSSINOW loves dancing, skiing, and playing soccer and softball. She was in the fifth grade when she wrote "Hiccups." She lives in Maine. *(p. 62)*

EDGAR ALLAN POE (1809–1849) had a worldwide influence on literature as the creator of the detective story and other forms of storytelling, like his highly musical poems and narratives. The list of his famous poems is long, but must include "The Raven," "Annabel Lee," and "The Bells." *(p. 24)*

IAN PULLEN was in fifth grade when he wrote "Calm Pond," which is based on his exciting experiences on the 10 acres of woods and fields that surround his home in Maine. His favorite sports are basketball and base-ball, and he enjoys playing the drums. *(p. 73)*

LIZ ROSENBERG was born and raised on Long Island, New York. She has published many books for children and adults. Her most recent anthologies of poems for young people are *Earth-Shattering Poems* (Henry Holt, 1998) and *The Invisible Ladder* (Henry Holt, 1996). She works as a visiting poet and teaches English and creative writing at the State University of New York at Binghamton. *(p. 59)*

JUDITH STEINBERGH is a poet, lyricist, and teacher of poetry. She has been working with student writers of all ages for more than 25 years. Judith's books include *Reading and Writing Poetry: A Professional Guide for Teachers, K–4* (Scholastic, 1994). She co-produced the award-winning *Where I Come From, Songs and Poems from Many Cultures* (Talking Stone Press). *(p. 69)*

MARK VINZ was born in Rugby, North Dakota, but grew up in Minneapolis and in the Kansas City area. Since 1968 he has taught in the English department of Moorhead State University in western Minnesota. He lives in Moorhead with his wife; they have two grown daughters. Vinz's poems have appeared in many magazines and anthologies. His two books of poetry are *Climbing the Stairs* (Spoon River Poetry Press, 1983) and *Mixed Blessings* (New Rivers Press). *(p. 54)*

ANNE WALDMAN was drawn to poetry at an early age, and today is known as an energetic performance poet. She published her first book of poems, *On The Wing*, in 1966, two years after graduating from college. In 1974 she helped establish the Naropa Institute in Boulder, Colorado, and has been a teacher there ever since. *(p. 45)*

WALT WHITMAN (1819–1892) is best known for *Leaves of Grass*, his monumental work of free verse. The "good gray poet" was deeply affected by the Civil War, particularly by his experiences as a volunteer nurse to wounded soldiers from both sides. He lived his last 19 years in Camden, New Jersey, revising *Leaves of Grass*. *(p. 46)*

ELINOR WYLIE (1885–1928) was born in New Jersey but published her first collection of poems anonymously in England in 1912. Although her literary career was brief, it is notable for two well-received volumes of poetry, *Nets to Catch the Wind* and *Black Armour*. Her *Collected Poems* (Knopf) was published four years after her death. *(p. 67)*

# INDEX

N.V. Edris

I DIDN'T START OUT TO BE A POET. I started out as a kid in New Jersey who had two major goals in life: to survive one more year of delivering newspapers without being attacked by Ike, the one-eyed, slobbering, crazed mutt that lurked in the forsythia bushes at the top of the hill, and to become more than a weak-hitting, third-string catcher on our sorry Little League team. I failed at both.

At that point in my life, poetry meant no more to me than George Washington's wooden teeth or the chief exports of the Belgian Congo. I was "gifted" only on my birthday and Christmas. But, by some strange twist of fate, I was lucky enough to become a writer of poetry. I wish I could name the teacher or poet who turned me around, but I can't. I suspect, however, that it was poetry itself that showed me what poetry could be. Poetry changed my life by changing the way I looked at the world. I discovered what Phillip Booth meant when he wrote that poetry "changes the world slightly in favor of being alive and being human." Poetry has become my constant companion. I can't imagine my life without it.

# Books by Paul B. Janeczko

## Poetry Anthologies

*The Crystal Image,* Dell, 1977

*Postcard Poems,* Bradbury Press, 1979

*Don't Forget to Fly,* Bradbury Press, 1981

*Poetspeak: In Their Work, About Their Work,* Bradbury Press, 1983
    (also available in trade paperback from Collier Books/Macmillan)

*Strings: A Gathering of Family Poems,* Bradbury Press, 1984

*Pocket Poems,* Bradbury Press, 1985

*Going Over to Your Place,* Bradbury Press, 1986

*This Delicious Day,* Orchard Books, 1987

*The Music of What Happens,* Orchard Books, 1988

*The Place My Words are Looking For,* Bradbury Press, 1990

*Preposterous: Poems of Youth,* Orchard Books, 1991

*Looking for Your Name,* Orchard Books, 1993

*Wherever Home Begins,* Orchard Books, 1995

*I Feel a Little Jumpy Around You* (with Naomi Shihab Nye),
    Simon & Schuster, 1996

*Home on the Range: Cowboy Poems,* Dial, 1997

*Very Best (Almost) Friends,* Candlewick Press, 1998

*Stone Bench in an Empty Park,* Orchard Books, 2000

*Poetry Takes Shape: Concrete Poems,* Candlewick Press, 2001

## POETRY

*Brickyard Summer,* Orchard Books, 1989

*Stardust Otel,* Orchard Books, 1993

*That Sweet Diamond: Baseball Poems,* Atheneum, 1998

## FICTION

*Bridges to Cross,* Macmillan, 1986

*Young Indiana Jones and the Pirates' Loot* (written as J.N. Fox), Random House, 1994

## NONFICTION

*Loads of Codes and Secret Ciphers,* Macmillan, 1984

*Poetry from A to Z: A Guide for Young Writers,* Bradbury Press, 1994

*A Scholastic Guide: How to Write Poetry,* Scholastic, 1999

## BOOKS FOR TEACHERS

*Favorite Poetry Lessons,* Scholastic, 1998

*Teaching Ten Fabulous Forms of Poetry,* Scholastic, 2000

# CREDITS

"What's In a Word" used by permission of the author.

"Edgar Allan Poe" by E.C. Bentley reproduced with permission of Curtis Brown Ltd., London, on behalf of the Estate of E.C. Bentley. Copyright E.C. Bentley.

"Things That Go Away and Come Back Again" used by permission of the author. Copyright 1970 by Anne Waldman.

"A History of Pets" from *Stopping by Home*. Copyright 1988 by David Huddle. Used by permission of the author.

"A History of the Faulty Shoes" used by permission of the author.

"How to Get Out of Homework" used by permission of the author.

"When I'm Alone I..." used by permission of the author.

"Grandmother" used by permission of the author.

"Hiccups" used by permission of the author.

"Sea Lullaby" from *Collected Poems* by Elinor Wylie. Copyright 1921 by Alfred A. Knopf Inc. and renewed 1949 by William Rose Benet. Reprinted by permission of the publisher.

"Mitten Dreams" used by permission of the author.

"Crocodile" used by permission of the author.

"Calm Pond" used by permission of the author.

"Cottontail" by George Bogin. Used by permission of the Estate of George Bogin.

"Niagra" from *Verse* by Adelaide Crapsey. Copyright 1922 by Algernon S. Crapsey and renewed 1950 by The Adelaide Crapsey Foundation. Reprinted by permission of Alfred A. Knopf Inc.

Poems by Paul B. Janeczko are used with the author's permission.

Writing tips are used with authors' permission.